# PRAISE FOR *A BO*

'*A Book for Life* is a treasure trove of wisdom from various traditions, ranging from Shamanism to Buddha's philosophy, and Zen to Western philosophy, all of which are intertwined with a plethora of ancient parables. Serving as a lighthouse, Jo's book is a guide to discovering one's aptitude along the journey of life, towards the goal suitable to each person's disposition and mental proclivities. I highly recommend this book.'
– Geshe Dorji Damdul, Former Translator to H.H. the Dalai Lama, Director, Tibet House, Cultural Center of H.H. the Dalai Lama, New Delhi

'Spiritual intelligence has arrived! A fresh, compelling and practical guide to the inner peace and creative power within each one of us.'
– Alberto Villoldo PhD, bestselling author of *One Spirit Medicine* and Shaman, Healer and Sage

'A must-read packed full of aha moments.'
– Naomie Harris OBE, Actor

'The most exciting book to be published for years, this is a guide to the art of life – it is absolutely beautiful. Start now!'
– Kate Reardon, Editor in Chief, *The Times LUXX Magazine*

'Life changing on every level.'
– Trinny Woodall, Founder of Trinny London

# A BOOK FOR LIFE

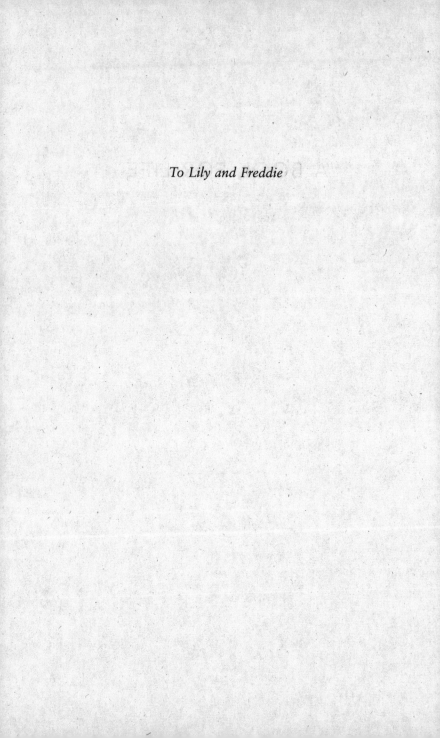

*To Lily and Freddie*

# A BOOK FOR LIFE

10 Steps to Spiritual Wisdom,
a Clear Mind and Lasting Happiness

## JO BOWLBY

First published in Great Britain in 2021 by Yellow Kite
An imprint of Hodder & Stoughton
An Hachette UK company

This paperback edition published in 2022

5

A CIP catalogue record for this title is available from the British Library

Paperback ISBN 978 1 529 34020 4
eBook ISBN 978 1 529 34018 1
Audiobook ISBN 978 1 529 34019 8

Typeset in Sabon MT by Palimpsest Book Production Ltd, Falkirk, Stirlingshire

Printed and bound in Great Britain by Clays Ltd, Elcograf S.p.A.

Hodder & Stoughton policy is to use papers that are natural, renewable
and recyclable products and made from wood grown in sustainable forests.
The logging and manufacturing processes are expected to conform
to the environmental regulations of the country of origin.

Yellow Kite
Hodder & Stoughton Ltd
Carmelite House
50 Victoria Embankment
London EC4Y 0DZ

www.yellowkitebooks.co.uk

# Contents

# Introduction

*Adventure is not outside man; it is within.*
– George Eliot

Of all the amazing things we can learn at school, how to be happy is not one of them. The focus is more on expanding the mind, rather than understanding it; and preparing you for what you want to do in life, rather than how you want to be. Happiness is treated more as a by-product of life or, like luck, an uncontrollable disposition that you are either blessed with or not. But that is not true. We all have the potential to have a very happy life, it is just a matter of learning how.

In this book I share what I consider to be the best life-enhancing skills that I have learnt from my time spent with some extraordinary wise men and women around the world over the last thirty years: Shamans living high in the Andes, medicine men and women in the Amazon rainforest, Buddhist scholars in India, mystics, gurus, philosophers and psychologists, all dedicated to sharing their wisdom on the art of life. Through these encounters I was able to gather a body of timeless wisdom which has underpinned my client work as a Shaman and spiritual coach/mentor over the last fifteen years.

I have always been the type of person who likes to find the point of something, quickly. I was the child, much to my teachers' irritation, who always asked, 'Why?' A born sceptic, I like proof not hearsay. This is perhaps what drew me to the ancient spiritual traditions. They don't ask you to believe anything or care whether you consider yourself spiritual or not. There are no rules, just maps to guide you so you don't get lost in the mind's labyrinth. They are there to support you in your own experience.

These ancient teachings are not the cute overused adages we see on car bumper stickers, but empowering insights and highly effective practices which can be life-changing. They come from experts who devoted their lives to understanding not just what makes us tick, but what makes a truly good life.

This book is my cherry-pickings from an enormous body of work. You might like to see it as a crib sheet or an executive summary. You will find everything that you need to create an empowering skillset to help you navigate life's inevitable twists and turns, allowing you to thrive in the good times and quickly recover when life knocks you off balance.

I have included lots of quick and easy practices for when you feel anxious, stressed, overwhelmed or mentally frayed, as well as gentle steps to guide you back to a deep sense of connection when you feel alone, hollow, lost or depressed.

This is not an empty promise. Everything in this book has been tried and tested over thousands of years. The practices work, and this is why more and more people are turning to the ancient spiritual traditions to help them flourish in their lives today.

The book is divided into two parts. The first part is an overview introducing Spiritual Intelligence, or SQ; a wisdom of life we recognise in the great sages and spiritual teachers that we are all able to develop. It is the missing ingredient to lasting happiness. Using ancient maps, I will paint a picture of our inner world landscape. Knowing this is a game changer because, regardless of the life we lead or the world we come from, our happiness and, for that matter, our entire mental well-being is entirely dependent on our state of mind.

The second part leads you through the actual process of how to develop your Spiritual Intelligence – the ten steps to gaining spiritual wisdom, a clear mind and lasting happiness.

## About the Process

*What we achieve inwardly will change outer reality.*
– Plutarch

The SQ Process is an adventure in self-discovery which opens up you to you and brings you face-to-face with everything that influences, affects and inhibits you; all the stories and personal fears which limit you and keep your world small. Until we can get ourselves and all our stuff out of the way, we will never see anything except for the limitations of our reality from our own perspective. To really come alive and embrace the magnitude and magnificence of life, we first have to let go of some of our unconscious safety blankets.

When most people think of a 'process', they think of something which is linear, with a set starting point and finishing line. A beginning and an end. But when it comes to a process of self-discovery, there is no end point where we can say, 'OK, I'm done and dusted, I now know everything there could possibly be to know about myself and life.' We are constantly evolving. We are not finite.

The SQ Process has a similar flow to the ancient medicine wheel, variations of which are used in many traditions to guide the seeker on a personal journey of development and transformation. It is made up of a series of steps and practices. It is a circle of letting go and bringing in, of facing fears so we can tap back into our own power of vision and feel safe to let our imagination fly. Each time we go around the wheel each layer becomes easier and the work faster.

The SQ Process takes you through ten core steps which will give you an insight into understanding why you are the way you are and how to become the person you want to be:

- Step One is about letting go of all the stories and beliefs we have about ourselves which keep us tethered to the past.
- Step Two digs a little deeper and goes into the shadows of our psyche, where our fears live, and empowers us to face them head-on.
- Step Three uncovers all the different masks we hide behind, because only then can we embrace our individuality and start dancing to our own drumbeat.
- Step Four is about coming off autopilot so that we are not left wondering where the day, year or life went.
- Step Five helps us to see that reality is not fixed, but, like a kaleidoscope, it morphs depending on which lens we use.
- Step Six teaches us that nothing in life is permanent and everything, from our own bodies to nature, is in a constant state of change.

- Step Seven is about being able to tap into your inner stillness, even in the midst of the chaos of daily life.
- Step Eight will show you how to read and direct energy, how to avoid having your energy depleted and how to replenish when you need more.
- Step Nine reveals how through nature we can find a profound connection which allows us to transcend our own life and rediscover a sense of awe.
- Step Ten is about becoming the author of your own destiny – understanding that we are all the hero in our own epic tale.

Throughout Part Two there are a range of exercises and practices taken from different spiritual traditions as well as modern-day psychology. The meditations are, in the main, from Buddhism and the reflections and questions of self-enquiry are typically Zen. Some are to help you in the moment, while others are questions to reflect on. The Shamanic exercises take us into a moment of ritual and ceremony, evoking something deep and heartfelt within us. They are designed to help us to break through the hold of the intellect, so we can get to a place beyond words. They are incredibly powerful and can shift the energy around an issue or belief without the need to intellectually understand it.

The SQ Process is something we can all do at any stage in our lives, wherever we are, whatever we are doing. It is really the ultimate adventure; a personal odyssey we all need to take if we wish to find our own voice, step into our own power and live life to the full.

Remember that this is a process and you will need to take an active part. It won't just happen to you. Set an intention as to what you want to gain from the process and from developing your own Spiritual Intelligence. This is really important – an intention gives you direction and is something to remind you when you are in the process why you are doing it. Your intention becomes a personal mantra, it brings both meaning and purpose.

# PART ONE

---

## Mind Matters

# The Ultimate Intelligence

*When I went to school, they asked me what I wanted to be when I grew up. I wrote down 'happy'. They told me I didn't understand the assignment, and I told them they didn't understand life.*

– John Lennon

When asked what the purpose of life is, His Holiness the Dalai Lama simply replied, 'to be happy'. It may seem a bit of a glib and insubstantial response to such an earnest question, but isn't happiness what we all want and strive for? Nobody wants to suffer, and if you strip back why we do everything we do, it is pretty much all driven by the hope or belief that it may lead to happiness, whatever that might mean to each of us.

To be clear, His Holiness is not talking about the momentary happiness which comes from buying an ice cream or a Ferrari. Nor is he talking about the happiness you get when you take a short break from the humdrum of daily life. He is referring to a deep and profound happiness; an inner peace, a strong sense of well-being that underpins all of your life, throughout your life, in good times and bad. This is true happiness.

You may be thinking that this is a nice ideal, but a pretty unrealistic dream for anyone living with the pressures of modern life. But the truth is that it is within all of our grasps – each and every one of us – regardless of whether we live in a palace or a prison cell.

We can all achieve this blissful inner stillness and deep-rooted happiness His Holiness the Dalai Lama is referring to by developing something innate in all of us called 'Spiritual Intelligence'. Contrary to its name, it has nothing to do with religion. Nor does it have anything to do with faith, hope or belief. It does, however, have everything to do with seriously enhancing our total well-being and giving us what we need to have a happy, fulfilling and meaningful life. Once developed, Spiritual Intelligence gives us an empowering knowledge, not only of ourselves, but of the nature of life itself, and this revelation, when it comes to our happiness, is a game changer. It is like understanding the magician's trick. Once you know how the trick is done, you can still enjoy the illusion, but it can no longer fool you.

We are not taught anything about Spiritual Intelligence at school. Most people know little about it or what it can offer us. But the fact is that it has been around for thousands of years; an open secret which has been held by all the ancient spiritual traditions.

We might learn bits and pieces of it here and there, just by living through the ups and downs of life, but we are really only forced to develop it when we have a life crisis, a loss or a tragedy. But, it shouldn't matter whether we are on a roll and finding life a breeze, or in a mess doing our best to just make it through the day, living life without Spiritual Intelligence is as unnecessary a challenge as jumping into a turbulent sea without first learning how to swim. Not knowing about it is definitely a wasted opportunity, as by developing our own Spiritual Intelligence we gain a valuable advantage in life.

Another way to see Spiritual Intelligence is spirituality put into action, which gives us a practical and effective skillset to enhance the great times and get us swiftly though the tough times. It is the core intelligence which runs through all spiritual traditions, as well as the modern schools of psychology. It is the foundation stone which supports our mental and emotional health, because it helps us in understanding everything – from how our life is dictated by our private inner world (aka the mind) to our ability to transcend our own life and see our place in a bigger picture. Most of all, it is about realising that although we like to think of ourselves as independent beings, none of us actually is. Even the yogi sitting in his little cave high in the Himalayas is dependent on the river for water, the cave for shelter and the air for breath. Because we are all part of the web of life, we are all part of a planetary cooperative, and our relationship and interdependence with both nature and our fellow human beings is crucial to our overall well-being.

Unlike Intellectual and Emotional Intelligence, which gauge our ability to acquire and process the day-to-day stuff in our lives, Spiritual Intelligence is the understanding of life itself. One way of seeing it is if you imagine yourself sitting watching a play in a theatre. Your intellect is helping you to make sense of the plot, whereas your emotions are letting you engage with the characters and the story. Spiritual Intelligence encompasses the two but also means you can see everything which goes on behind the scenes. It is like having an access-all-areas pass. If you see Intellect as left brain and Emotions as right brain, Spiritual Intelligence is the whole brain. Really it is the sum of all other intelligences. You could call it the 'ultimate intelligence' and the good news is, we all have the seed of this intelligence within us. For exactly the same reasons we might exercise regularly to develop our muscles to keep our body healthy, we need to develop our Spiritual Intelligence to keep our mind healthy.

## Knowing Your Mind

*I will not let anyone walk through my mind with their dirty feet.*
– Mahatma Gandhi

If we want to look after our mental well-being, the first thing we have to do is get to know our own mind. When we think about the mind, we tend to think about what's on it rather than the actual mind itself, which is a little like focusing on the clouds and ignoring the sky. The mind is much more than simply a house for our intellectual thoughts and academic prowess, it is the very essence of us – it is our heart and soul.

Our whole world – absolutely everything to do with our life and how we live it – is governed by our mind. Every thought, fear, emotion, belief and perception that we have is controlled by it, which, in effect, makes our mind our intangible and invisible boss. It is certainly elusive in nature. Not just because it goes by a number of different names – the psyche, the inner self, the internal world, 'awareness' and 'consciousness' – but also because no one can quite agree on what exactly the mind is or, for that matter, *where* it is.

If we are asked to point to where we think it is in our body, most of us would probably point to our foreheads. It feels like it is possibly in our brain, or at least within our skull somewhere behind our eyes. But if a neurosurgeon were to open your head up and have a little poke around your brain, they wouldn't find it. Perhaps because the mind is not the brain in the same way as the evening news is not the television. Just as we need a TV or a similar device to access the programme, we need the brain to access the mind. And just as the flashiest TV is pointless without programmes to stream through it, our brain is pretty pointless without the experience of our mind.

Quite simply, without our mind we cease to exist. Without our mind, everything disappears.

One of the reasons the mind remains elusive is because it is not a finite organ like the brain, but a free-flowing energy. It is a conscious energy which gives us our personal experience of life, and it is maybe the very thing which connects us to a universal objective intelligence, a universal consciousness. The mind is the personal part of this objective, pure consciousness which holds our experience of life. Where the two merge is as indefinable as knowing exactly where the sky merges into space.

When it comes to our minds, there is one thing everyone does agree on, and that is that we all have one and life is immeasurably better when it is working with us rather than against us.

## Too Busy to Be

*Beware the barrenness of a busy life.*
– Socrates

The flip side to the mind-blowing advancements we have made over the last century is that, rather than life getting easier and happier, it is becoming increasingly stressful and overwhelming. More and more of us are struggling to cope with the pressures, the noise and the overwhelming pace of modern life. We live in a world which never switches off and there is little to no respite from the constant 'doing'. Busy is seen as good and a sign that we are valued and needed. Whether it is an impenetrable to-do list, balancing work and home life, bringing up a family or a day of non-consequential but seemingly essential appointments, we are all busy. We are constantly juggling our needs, desires and expectations. There is a collective belief that if we are flat out, we are not only important, but we are doing well in life. Busy is considered normal and a good way to live.

The problem is we are living in a speeding world that carries on getting faster and faster year on year like a runaway train. In a bid to keep up, we are starting to resemble crazed children on a permanent sugar high. Wherever we are at, whatever we have achieved, it is not enough. We need more. We need our fix. We are perpetually looking forward to the next thing. There is an unrelenting pressure from others, as well as ourselves, to do more, be more, make more. Our ability or desire to concentrate for long periods has gone out the window – we like to have everything in short bursts and quick soundbites. We need to get to the point quickly so we can get on with whatever is next. We are in a permanent unsustainable state of alert. We are addicted to constant stimulation and we don't know how to come down from always doing something or always being entertained, and the stress on our mind, body and soul is taking its toll.

Our modern lifestyle is coming at the expense of our health, in particular our mental health. Our minds never get a chance to rest. We are mentally exhausted. Anyone with young children knows that an overtired child equates to tantrums and tears. Well, we are no different, except, unlike the child, we can learn to decipher our own emotional signs. When our emotions fray, our sleep pattern goes awry, our moods start to get darker and we find ourselves barking at everyone around us, we have a choice. We can either ignore the signs and keep going until the side effects literally stop us, or we can take it as a signal that it is time to take stock and make some adjustments.

If you can't remember the last time you had a full night's sleep or the last time you watched a movie without checking your phone every five minutes, there is a high chance you are caught in fight or flight: a primal survival state of emergency.

A lot of people are talking about fight or flight nowadays because it is widely accepted to be a common cause behind a range of mental and physical illnesses. Post-traumatic stress disorder (PTSD), anxiety, chronic fatigue syndrome and insomnia, as well as gut issues, are just a few examples of its effects. Also known as 'acute stress response', it is the body's automatic response to anything it perceives as life-threatening. It allows us, for what was only intended to be a brief moment in time, to be superhuman. It heightens our awareness to acute levels and gives us superfast reflexes and speed, so we have the best chance of fleeing from danger. It is exactly the same survival reflex we can see throughout the animal kingdom, except there is one crucial difference. In this instance, our evolved mind is actually our downfall. Our ability to remember and to analyse means it can be as harmful as it is helpful for us.

Imagine, if you will, a young zebra calmly grazing with the rest of its herd on a huge open plain when, all of a sudden, a lion starts to make chase. With the sense of an imminent threat, the fight or flight reflex is triggered in each of the herd. The young zebra's heart rate rises, its breathing quickens, its blood gets re-directed away from digesting grass, as well as its other vital organs, to its muscles and limbs, so it is able to react and flee for its life. If it is lucky enough to outrun the lion, as soon as it senses the threat is over, its stress hormones will drop and its system will return to normal. It may do a violent body shake as if removing the fear energy and then, in a matter of moments, it will go back to calmly eating grass as if nothing ever happened.

We, on the other hand, have lost this art of recovery. We can't shake the stress off quite so easily and it is all because of our ability to conceptualise. Although most of us are unlikely to come under threat from a lion, the fight or flight reflex can be triggered from any perceived traumatic event. It is a primal system which doesn't differentiate between a lion on the attack and a yelling boss. Our ability to replay a threat to our lives – real or otherwise – over and over in our minds means we remain triggered. Our stress levels stay elevated and we remain locked in a state of high alert. Our bodies are braced ready to react like a soldier on the front line. The effect is physically, mentally and emotionally exhausting; it literally starts to wear us down. (Later in the book

I will give you some exercises which are really effective at getting the whole system to completely relax at a deep level.)

This triggered fight or flight reflex helps to explain why many of us find it so hard to get our minds to stop racing and switch off. The average human has over 2,000 thoughts an hour, which is over twice as many as the breaths we take in the same time. It is tiring just thinking about it. Welcome to what Buddhists call the 'monkey mind'. The experts reckon we have between 60,000 and 90,000 thoughts a day, which makes for a very busy monkey. We are constantly thinking, but rarely do we see any of our thoughts through to the end. Something within the thought makes us think of something else and off we go randomly swinging from one thought to the next, and the next.

Next time you catch yourself lost in a stream of thoughts, try retracing back through each one to see how you ended up there. Find the original thought and see if you can hold it long enough to actually finish it. This is a powerful little exercise in taming the monkey mind. It can also be quite fun seeing how random the leaps in thought can be!

Unlike us, our ancestors had no choice but to abide by the laws of nature. However, this meant they had the chance to relax at the end of the day. They didn't have luxuries like electricity, so they had to follow the circadian rhythm. The equivalent of their TV was sitting around watching the fire they slept by, letting their minds stretch out and unwind from the stimulation of the day. They had a natural opportunity to harmonise, to find themselves again within the hustle and bustle of their daily lives. Unlike our ancestors, we have to make time in our diaries to do this. One of the greatest gifts we can give ourselves is to stop for a few moments in our day to simply check in on ourselves – to come back into the moment – because it is all too easy to lose ourselves, flying from one thing to the next in everyday life, to get lost in the doing. It is important to take time in our day to press pause, so that, even if it is just for one moment, we can find our feet, we can ground ourselves, we can land.

## Deep breathing meditation

Here is a simple one-minute meditation to help you catch your breath:

- Place one hand on your stomach and your other hand on your heart.
- Close your eyes and start to breathe deeply, so you first feel your stomach filling up into your hand and then you feel your breath extending up to your chest.
- As you exhale, first let the air release from the chest and then from the stomach. So, both hands are moving with each breath.
- On the inhalation the stomach hand moves first, followed by the chest hand, and on the exhalation the chest hand moves first, followed by the stomach hand.
- As you inhale, imagine inhaling pure cleansing energy and letting it wash through every cell of your body.
- As you exhale, imagine letting go of all the stress and toxins from your system.

For some, stopping takes more courage than continually doing. We can find a sanctuary in 'the doing' which means we can avoid ever being with ourselves. In fact, many of us spend most of our lives running away from ourselves. We don't want to face ourselves for fear of what we might find or, worse, let in, because it might create a space for the internal voices (yes, we all have them) to start up with their commentary on how we are getting life wrong, how we are not good enough. Maybe if we slow down then everyone will realise we have no idea what we are doing.

## It's Personal

*Knowing others is wisdom, knowing yourself is enlightenment.*

– Lao Tzu

More and more of us, regardless of age, gender, culture, religion or status, are falling victim to either an existential crisis or debilitating stress and depression. Mental illness does not discriminate. Mental and emotional well-being is now a regular leading news story as some of those who epitomise success and good fortune from across the board are opening up about their personal struggles with depression, trauma, anxiety or despair, feeling lost, overwhelmed, empty or questioning the meaning or purpose of their lives.

Anyone who has ever struggled with any of these hard-to-bear fears or emotions knows that heaven and hell are not exclusive to an afterlife, they are states of mind which exist in all of us right now as we live and breathe. Being consumed with an anxiety or depression can be a living hell, just as being loved-up or enjoying a perfect moment can be heaven. The state of our mind has total control over whether we flourish or flounder, and directly impacts the quality of our life. By developing our Spiritual Intelligence, we stop having to fear our own mind and it becomes a trusted ally.

Mental disorders are subjective. For each person the cause and the severity are different. For one person, depression can feel like a black cloud which drains the colour out of life, while for another depression can be so cripplingly exhausting they dread getting out of bed. It doesn't really matter how many labels we choose to use to differentiate the range of illnesses, they are simply different names to describe the fact that our mind is struggling to find its balance. They are all forms of mental unease and signs that we have come off-kilter for one reason or another. The one common denominator in all mental illness is the mind. This is why becoming familiar with the nature of the mind and how it works is crucial to our overall well-being.

Understanding the human condition is eye-opening. Being able to go beyond our habitual behaviour and clearly see how our minds manipulate and control everything we do is life-changing. Most of us never turn our focus to the actual mind itself until something goes wrong. Up until that point we tend to give our mind free rein to think what it wants when it wants. It doesn't occur to us to question it. So, when our mind spooks at a minor situation or forms a choir of voices to tell us how pathetic or useless we are, we take it as fact. We completely trust that whatever our mind tells us is an accurate and objective representation of reality, and it is this blind belief which is at the root of a lot of our mental anguish.

Our mind as we know it is neither pure nor objective, because when we think of the mind we are thinking of what's in it, not the mind itself; the clouds in the sky, not the sky itself. It is stamped with our personal experience and interpretation of pretty much everything – not just from our own lifetime, but also beliefs and conditionings we have inherited. Plastered in our mind, like the clouds in the sky, are the footprints of past reactions to past experiences, each one affecting how we interpret the world around us and how we experience life.

If you grew up playing with My Little Pony and dreaming of one day owning your own horse, a best friend with whom you will have lots of adventures, your feelings about horses are going to be in stark contrast to the person who as a child was kicked or bitten by an angry horse. Or the person who was forced to enjoy riding simply because their parents did and spent a childhood being told how lucky they were. How we see horses is entirely based on what kind of experience we have or haven't had with them. These experiences and how we interpret them become emotional imprints. Just like dirty footprints, they mark our mind and will continue to hold an influence over us until we remove them. As we go through the process of developing our Spiritual Intelligence, we start to recognise and clear these imprints and, as we do so, we start to live less at the mercy of our mind. We cease being thrown about like tumbleweed by every thought, fear and emotion.

As soon as we cotton on to the fact that what is on our mind is not objective but made up of personal interpretations, we can start to reclaim control. Because if the mind is subjective then it is malleable. It means our mind is not a fait accompli which we have to manage or endure. We have the power to not just tame and train our mind but actually befriend it, which means we have the power to flourish with its support.

We can't stop negative emotions from ever getting a grip on us again or avoid moments when the gaggle of voices in our head catches us unawares. However, there are plenty of things we can do to disempower them and regain control.

One easy but very effective way to break any toxic thought pattern or to shut up the voices in your head is the five senses meditation. It doesn't matter where you are; it can be done in bed, on the bus or during a meeting. By going through the five senses – vision, hearing, smell, taste and touch – you effectively come out of the virtual reality of your thoughts and into your body for just long enough that it is impossible to go back to the exact place you left off. You can do this meditation without even putting this book down.

## Five senses meditation

- First, look around and in your head name anything you can see: a chair, a window, a red car . . . five or six things you can see right now.
- Then notice what the furthest sound is that you can hear. It may be traffic, the sound of an aeroplane or somebody's voice.
- Next, notice what the nearest sound is that you can hear. This could be a bird outside your window or, if you are very quiet, you may be able to hear a sound in your ears or your own breath.
- Then notice what you can smell. If you can't smell anything, smell the back of your hand or your sleeve.

- Now notice what you can taste in your mouth.
- Finally, notice how your body feels in the seat, the bed or wherever you are.

This whole exercise needn't take more than thirty seconds, but you can string it out for as long as you want. Once you have finished, feel free to go back to whatever it was you were thinking, if you can. The thought pattern will not have the same hold on you the second time round. This is an exercise that you can do as and when you remember to. It can be done as often as you want, on the hour every hour or whenever it is helpful. Coming out of our heads and back into our body is an effective way of creating some distance between our self and any negative self-talk.

## Potholes on the Path

> *Experience is not what happens to you, it is what you do with what happens to you.*
> – Aldous Huxley

Spiritual Intelligence definitely gives us an advantage in life, but it doesn't mean that even when developed we have a free pass from our share of trials and troubles. As much as we might like to think otherwise, we cannot control what life drops on our doorstep. However, we do have full control over how we react to it. How we let life shape us is our choice. We can take it as a given that part of life's course is to continually chuck us challenges and it is inevitable that there are going to be times in all our lives when we are not only going to get knocked off balance but floored. Our happiness and our well-being are not pinned on never coming off balance, but Spiritual Intelligence gives us an empowering resilience when our life turns south, which means we have the ability to recover fast.

One of the most powerful realisations which comes from developing our Spiritual Intelligence is accepting that nobody is flawless, not even the most esteemed spiritual teachers of our time.

When we develop our Spiritual Intelligence, we realise that we alone are responsible for our life, and rather than this being a harsh truth, it is actually both liberating and empowering. We get to choose how we live our life, not someone or something else. For this reason, the better informed we are, the better chance we have of our life panning out the way we want it to. Spiritual Intelligence puts our destiny firmly back in our own hands. It reminds us we are the authors of our own story and not simply a bit-part player in someone else's.

# But What Does It Mean?

*Man cannot discover new oceans unless he has the courage to lose sight of the shore.*
– André Gide

Spirituality has become burdened with so many different connotations and misconceptions that it's hard to know what someone actually means when they refer to being 'spiritual' or having a spiritual practice. On that note, it's just as confusing working out what someone means when they claim not to have a spiritual bone in their body. Nowadays the term can refer to a smorgasbord of schools, traditions, practices and processes, from the ancient to the brand new.

Spiritual speak doesn't help matters either. Aside from the new-age phrases and meaningful looks which have carried through from the Summer of Love in the sixties, it is overflowing with metaphors which, by their very nature, are open to interpretation. As with any world, spirituality also has its own lingo. However, unlike most lingo, which acts as a shorthand and once explained is easily understood, spiritual speak tends to do the exact opposite. It is made up of enigmatic words and phrases which can do more to confuse than to clarify. Ask a hundred spiritual practitioners to define 'enlightenment', 'higher consciousness', 'awakened', 'awareness', 'true nature' and 'being at one with the universe' and there is a strong chance you will come away none the wiser.

So it is understandable that the word 'spiritual' has driven many to avoid it altogether or to keep their interest a secret for fear that they aren't going to be taken seriously and simply be dismissed as woo-woo, fanciful and out of touch with the real world. Silicon Valley is trying to give spirituality a makeover, replacing the flowery tones with cool, edgy definitions, so now, instead of it being cloaked in poetic metaphors, it is being dynamically dressed in techspeak like 'mind-hacking', 'subconscious reprogramming' and 'life upgrades'.

It is good the language is opening up and spirituality is being explained in a way which can appeal to a larger audience. It re-affirms the fact that the traditions hold a timeless wisdom which remains relevant for all of us here and now in the modern world even with its cutting-edge technology. It reflects the value those at the top of their game put into developing their own SQ.

Much of the new packaging promotes how these ancient practices can help us to achieve more, to do better at work and manifest abundance in all areas of our life.

However, although we can use spiritual practices to focus on our goals, spirituality offers much more than simply manifesting a better job or partner. In a bid to make it more widely marketable we might be throwing the proverbial baby out with the bath water. Because goals do not sate the soul. They do not bring anything more than a momentary happiness. We know this. If they did, then those who personify success would be spared from ever feeling empty or depressed. To simply use the spiritual teachings as a goal-facilitator confines spirituality to the very paradigm from which we are looking to shift, to transcend. Using it for these purposes is like using a space shuttle to do your weekly food shop.

Meditation is a powerful and valuable antidote for anxiety, and it is a true sanctuary for when we feel overwhelmed with life, but its gifts extend far beyond being simply a maintenance or coping tool. Meditation is mind-opening: it helps us transcend the daily stuff; it is how we can pan out from the micro of our personal lives through the macro to the infinite of unknown potential.

Metaphors evoke something in us deeper than intellectual understanding. They help us to access a place beyond words. They can ignite our heart and soul. There is purpose to the poetic phrases and sweeping broad brushes rather than precise unequivocal language, and that is because spirituality is subjective. It is about experience, our personal experience. We can identify with someone else's experience, resonate and be deeply inspired by their story. Ultimately though, to really reap the infinite benefits, the experience has to be our own. To intellectually understand the benefits of closing your eyes for twenty minutes a day in meditation has no value unless you actually give it a go.

If you strip away all the embellishments – the rituals and the metaphors, exotic or otherwise – then, at its bare roots, spirituality is an adventure of self-discovery. And it is the most important adventure any of us can make. It is a process of realisation which shows us that there is so much more to life than the surface stuff we fixate on. We are like the baby who doesn't realise the packaging isn't the gift. At some point in our lives, be it through curiosity or crisis, a surface material existence can start to feel empty, even pointless, and we realise that in order to find any depth or meaning we must look beyond the shiny eye-catching wrapper.

Today, when a person talks about being spiritual, they are typically referring to one of the ancient traditions where practices such as meditation, and many others less mainstream, originated. They are not talking about religion. In fact, spirituality and religion are no longer one and the same. They are not interchangeable. Being spiritual or simply adopting some of the practices has no bearing on whether you are deeply religious, an atheist or somewhere in between. Nor does it require you to change your entire wardrobe to flowing robes, fill your house with crystals and bid namaste to everyone who passes you by. You do not need to subscribe to a church or a belief structure. That said, if you are religious, none of the ancient traditions or practices will interfere with your personal faith or beliefs. You can be spiritual and be religious; you can be spiritual and be an atheist; you can even be spiritual and be a scientist.

This may well make some scientists recoil, but science and spirituality are not dissimilar. They are both dedicated to the pursuit of understanding the world in which we live. In the case of science, it is the understanding of the world around us, and in the case of spirituality, understanding the world within us. One is objective, the other subjective. One is backed up by statistics, the other by lived experience.

## The Still Explorers

*The real voyage of discovery consists not in seeking new landscapes, but in having new eyes.*
– Marcel Proust

Throughout time there have always been folk who have seen the world a little differently from their community. Each generation has its loners and outsiders, whose curiosity and interests set them apart from the crowd, and it is probably safe to say that the first spiritual masters fitted into this category. They were the original intrepid explorers pushing frontiers into the unknown. The landscape they were interested in wasn't the world around them, but the inner world. The beginnings of spirituality stretch back over 30,000 years and the original spiritual masters were probably the Shamans. The Shaman was an integral part of every community – a sort of one-stop shop acting as psychologist, philosopher, life coach and healer. They were the wise person in the tribe, revered and feared and often considered other-worldly simply because their interest in the nature of life meant that they understood and perceived things the rest of the tribe didn't. The skills they spent time cultivating are skills innate to all of us.

As with the spiritual masters who followed, they saw beyond the trance of everyday living: studying and observing everything in a bid to make sense of our world and how we fit into it. While their peers went about their daily routines, caught up in the theatre of everyday life, the spiritual masters realised that much of our lives is just that – a show, an illusion most people take unquestioningly as reality. Their fascination lay in how the show, a collective illusion, came about and the suffering it caused everyone caught up in it.

They went about unpicking the very fabric of life, and in particular the human condition, in the same way a person might take apart a radio. They were the first to explore and map the different levels of the mind and realise how, like a puppeteer, it works behind the scenes controlling not only how we see life, but our very experience of life.

Although the nature of life may to this day remain a mystery to most people, the question of how to have a profoundly happy one was solved thousands of years ago by, among others, a man who found answers by sitting under a tree for forty-nine days without moving. For millennia these wise men and women have been idolised and revered like demigods, but although they were unquestionably extraordinary geniuses in their field, they didn't waft down to earth chaperoned by celestial beings. They were mere mortals, normal people like you and me. Like us, they were susceptible to the laws of nature; to life, to death and to suffering. They were exposed to the same situations and conditions as the people they lived amongst.

If you are wondering how on earth anybody, however wise or determined from so far back in history, can have insights or any experience that could be remotely relevant to your life today, the answer is simple. When it comes to our wants, our needs and our desires, absolutely nothing has changed. The stage may be very different, and we may not have the same immediate concerns of our ancestors or even our grandparents, but our want for happiness, to love and be loved, and a need to control our environment so we feel safe remain the same. We are no different than our ancestors from 30,000 years ago.

Regardless of all the extraordinary advancements we have made, the human condition has remained unchanged. Stress and anxiety are not new feelings. We are not the first to struggle with the darker human emotions. We are not the first to feel, at times, lost, empty or overwhelmed by life.

The fact that their discoveries and insights could really help people in all aspects of their own lives made the spiritual masters understandably very popular. They had come up with the answers to life and how to live it, so it was unsurprising that people came from far and wide to hear what they had to say. As their followings grew, schools and traditions formed. Some traditions formed from other traditions, schools split, but they all had a common goal: to share their expertise on life.

## Blueprints

*All truths are easy to understand once they are discovered; the point is to discover them.*

– Galileo Galilei

Thousands of years later and we are still turning to them in the hope that we too can benefit from their expertise on life and how to live it. Practices like mindful meditation and yoga are now pretty much mainstream. It is not surprising really – you only have to look at the knowing serenity and stillness on a Buddhist monk's face in meditation, to know the ancient traditions offer us something richer than money. As it is the exact opposite to how most of us feel on any given day, it makes a powerful advert for looking into what these traditions have to offer. There is no question that these practices really will go a long way to enhancing the quality of our life – even science is starting to accept this. But if you also study the original teachings which underpin these practices, you will be able not only to enhance your life, but have the power if you wish to change it.

The ancient teachings act as maps which explain the entire mind's landscape. Each school and tradition has its own map which has been drawn up over the years by devotees dedicated to showing us all how to navigate life and, in particular, how to avoid suffering. If you were to go by Malcolm Gladwell's rule – that if you practise a skill for 10,000 hours, you'll stand a good chance of becoming an expert in it – it comfortably makes them indisputable masters in this field. All the maps shine a light on an invisible landscape of the mind and give us tangible help in making sense of something which is intangible. This means that when our lives fall apart for whatever reason and our illusions of life are shattered, we do not have to flail around in a mind abyss forever lost and broken. We have the insights of the ancient masters to help pull us out and the practices to act as stepping stones so that we can recover our balance.

In essence, all the ancient spiritual traditions and the modern schools of psychology are saying the same thing, but most important of all they are all showing us how to get to the same place. It is just that their methods are different. As the Vietnamese Zen monk Thich Nhat Hanh says, 'the raft is not the shore'. The Buddhist map of the mind appeals to the cerebral as it goes into minute academic detail. It speaks to the intellect. The Shamans' blueprint, on the other hand, is much more flamboyant. It is full of colour and is quite literally alive as they use nature to depict and bring to life the inner landscape. It is visceral and it appeals to the senses. It speaks to the soul. Unlike most other traditions, up until recently their knowledge and practices were never written down. They were passed down orally, within the community, from grandparent to grandchild. They taught through stories and direct experience.

Today we are living in the golden age of information, which means that even though for centuries these teachings were confined to the monasteries or shared with only a select few, we now all have access to them. We don't have to don saffron, shave our heads or retreat solo into the rainforest; we can benefit from them wherever we are, whatever we are doing. The downside of this golden age is that there is so much information to plough through, the most valuable maps can remain hidden in plain sight. Unless you have some knowledge of what you are looking for, it is hard to know what is what. It can be genuinely confusing.

The SQ Process outlined in Part Two has been formed by bringing together the common themes shared by all the different maps, both old and new. It filters all the teachings down to their core components, gathering a range of different paths to create one clear road which you can follow. It is a timeless blueprint which explains in clear steps how to reignite joy and the imagination, and how to achieve a great life full of depth and free from anguish and suffering.

With this blueprint, we have to hand the information and insights that we need, so that we can understand and tame the very thing which is responsible for what kind of life we have.

## Remembering Freedom

*In the depth of winter, I finally learned that within me there*
*lay an invincible summer.*
– Albert Camus

At the core of all spirituality practices is freedom. The SQ Process
brings us to this freedom. When you think of freedom, you may
envisage yourself with arms outstretched in front of a huge expanse
of land or sea. Or you might have a sense of the freedom that
comes with having a mountain of cash at your disposal. Or perhaps
freedom for you is simply the ability to do as you choose: whatever
you wish whenever you wish.

However, none of these can guarantee us a sense of freedom,
not even for a moment. Because the harsh truth is, whether we
can do some or all of the above, we will not taste freedom if our
own minds aren't in agreement.

True freedom is a mind state. If our mind is upset, if it is full
of fear or negative self-talk, it really doesn't matter whether we
are sitting in paradise or we are surrounded by all the things we
ever dreamt of, we will not feel free. Our freedom is entirely
dependent on our state of mind. By developing our Spiritual
Intelligence, we can be truly free, regardless of where and how we
live.

The SQ Process leads us to freedom by reconnecting us to our
true nature – our pure mind. It is like the new home before we
fill it with all our personal belongings. Just as we can remove all
our stuff from said new home, so can we clear the emotional
baggage and all the clutter of beliefs and conditionings from our

mind. Every single one of us has a pure mind; it is our true, intrinsic nature. As the clouds can block our view of the sun, so can our imprints and ignorance of the nature of life keep us from seeing our true nature.

It is the 'you' which is untarnished and unscathed by life. The 'you' before your beliefs about life formed and anchored you to a way of being. However anxious, unhappy, angry or depressed we are, these ways of feeling are not part of our true nature. Think back to the clouds in the sky – they are not permanent, they pass by or we can learn how to vaporise them.

# PART TWO

———

## The SQ Process

# The Story of You

## The Mind Detox

*It is our mind, and that alone, that chains us or sets us free.*
— Dilgo Khyentse Rinpoche

Close your eyes for a moment and imagine your home stuffed to bursting with everything you have ever owned. Every drawer spilling over with all the things you have picked up over the years. Clothes going all the way back to the romper suits that you wore as a baby crammed into your wardrobes, and a seemingly endless display of family heirlooms covering every surface. Oh, and an attic and cellar, should you have them, piled high with boxes which you haven't looked through for years, if ever, with more of the same.

This hoarder's delight probably doesn't describe your home, but it may well describe your mind.

It is obvious that if we want to keep our home in good working order, we need to keep it at least vaguely clean and once in a while send the clothes we don't wear anymore off to the local charity shop, along with Aunt Agatha's cherished china cat collection. It doesn't occur to many of us, however, that stored in our mind is an ever-growing pile of beliefs and stories, some dating back to our childhood, which are having a direct influence on how we live our life right now. Giving our mind a detox is very different from sitting down with a fine-tooth comb and analysing what's on our mind piece by piece. Nor is it about downloading a mindful meditation app in a bid to help us find some respite from the chatter inside. For many of us, a mind detox is an overdue clear-out. Don't worry, this is not a painful exercise; in fact, quite the contrary. It is freeing and revitalising – like taking off a heavy backpack you weren't aware you were carrying.

This is the first step in the SQ Process – a chance to silence the internal noise and shed the stories which keep us from feeling fulfilled. It is learning how to deal with the toxins in our life and understanding that in the same way what we eat affects our body, so what we think affects our mind. Detoxing your mind is the first step in a personal adventure into understanding why you are the way you are and becoming the person you want to be. It demands the same inquisitiveness you had as a child – a want to know why, the curiosity to make you look behind your stories. Like all adventures, at times it will be challenging and you will need to dig deep. But the reward for showing a bit of courage in knocking down familiar old beliefs and patterns is a profound sense of freedom.

This is not about whitewashing your past or pretending events, painful or otherwise, didn't happen. It is not in our control to change an event that has happened, but the story we choose to wrap around them is. When you realise that suffering is not in the actual event but in the story you tell yourself about the event, your life will be transformed. How you choose to see an event is completely within your control. Unlike the event itself, the narrative you spin around it is not fact. It is your interpretation of the event.

We all want a happy life, and no one goes out looking for ways to suffer. So, when you realise that you dictate your own suffering, it is a game changer. It essentially means that suffering is a choice.

A Buddhist parable tells the story of two monks travelling together; one old, the other young. They are walking down a path when they come to a fast-running river with a strong current, where they find a young woman who is waiting on the riverbank afraid to cross on her own. When she sees the monks, she gets up and asks them for help. Without a word the old monk picks her up, carries her across the river and sets her down on the other side. The young monk is shocked that the old monk has broken a sacred vow without a moment's hesitation, but he says nothing, and they continue on their travels.

An hour passes, then two, then three. Finally, the now-agitated young monk can't contain his thoughts anymore and blurts out: 'You shouldn't have carried that woman. You broke the sacred vow we took as monks to never touch a woman.'

The old monk calmly replied, 'I set her down hours ago. Why are you still carrying her?'

Once you can see all the different stories you hoard in your mind, it is far easier and quicker to do ongoing maintenance. We alone are responsible for our mental hygiene and we have to wake up to the tirade of thoughts, opinions, judgements and concerns we feed it. The toxic self-sabotaging commentary of 'I am useless, stupid, not good enough, unlovable' achieves nothing except to drain the colour out of our life. This is simply a matter of a little discipline. In discipline there is freedom and, for a troubled mind, sanctuary.

The reason most of us never really question what's on our minds is because we think we *are* our mind. We see both as 'us'. But it is really important to be able to separate what's on our mind from the mind itself. Our thoughts are not our mind. They are not 'you' and you do not have to take them on without question. Just because you 'think' something or a particular thought comes into your mind, it doesn't mean you have to believe it. Having a thought does not make it a fact or true. Here is a little exercise which will show you what I mean.

Think of a majestic eagle circling silently high in the sky; take a moment to really see it. Now think of a beautiful full moon on a clear night; again, take a moment to picture it. Finally think of a huge bright yellow triangle. The observer of the eagle flying, the full moon and the yellow triangle is the same observer who observes the stream of thoughts you have all day long. In the same way you let the eagle fly in and out, you have control of the pile of your thoughts clogging your mind. You are not the eagle, or the full moon, or the yellow triangle, just as you are not any of the thoughts in your head. In the same way you consciously thought of those three things, you have to be conscious of the thoughts you are thinking. The key is to create space between you the observer and your thoughts. The more distance you create, the less hold they will have over you and the less chance you have of getting lost in them. This is also true when it comes to negative emotions. We like to embody emotions – 'I am angry', 'I am anxious', 'I am depressed'. Next time you catch yourself saying something like this, put some distance between yourself and the emotion. Watch the emotion in the same way Sir David Attenborough watches an interesting species. See it as its own life form which you do not have to hook into. Stand back and let it (the e-motion) pass through.

One of the most empowering things I learnt in my training was with a medicine man in the Amazon. He showed me that absolutely everything – from the thoughts in our head to the rainforest itself – is made up of energy. He was renowned as a strong and powerful healer who showed no interest whatsoever in someone's story. He didn't care about your problems in life or, for that matter, your dreams. His focus was solely on your energy flow and bringing it back into balance. He showed me that when our energy isn't flowing properly it can manifest as disease or mental anguish. He wasn't a miracle worker, he simply went about clearing a person's energy blocks in the same way you might remove rocks from a river. Once the energy is flowing properly, the body comes into balance and carries out any healing that is necessary. You don't have to go all the way to the Amazon to experience this. We all already have the ability to change our own energy. We do it every day of our lives: laughing with friends, a heated conversation, reading a sad story, going to the gym or a calming meditation. Each has an effect on our energy. The better we understand energy the more control we have over our lives.

There is an old, probably apocryphal, Native American story which illustrates this beautifully. Sitting around the campfire one evening, the old chief decides to tell his grandson about a terrible battle.

'This battle is fought between two wolves which live inside us all. One wolf is consumed with fear, self-loathing, worry and negative thoughts. The other wolf is courageous, confident, kind and passionate about life.'

The young boy thinks about it for a minute and, full of concern, asks, 'So which wolf wins?'

The chief replies, 'The one you feed.'

## What's in a Story?

*You may not control all the events that happen to you, but you can decide not to be reduced by them.*

– Maya Angelou

The whole world is made up of stories, or maybe better put, stories make our world exist. Stories bring our world to life for us. Quite simply, everything in life is a story. From the evening news with their opening lines: 'Our top story tonight', to the stories we tell about ourselves. History is also a story (the clue is in the name), and it is normally written through the eyes of the winners. Even those observing an event cannot help giving it a subjective slant.

Our personal stories, as with the global ones, help us to place ourselves in a great big abstract world, to connect and make heartfelt friendships with like-minded souls who see the world the same way we do. Stories bring us together and hold us together. Storytelling is an ancient human instinct. Stories help us to find the tribes we resonate with. We have the tribes we are born into – our family, our culture, our faith – and the tribes we choose ourselves – from our friends to our favourite football team. Each is bound by stories. There is something wonderful about listening to someone tell you about themselves and finding yourself resonating at a deep level. From the beginning of time humans have sat around the campfire telling each other stories. Stories can teach, inspire and comfort. They shape our reality. They are the golden threads which allow us to make sense of life and the world around us. They mark where we have come from and map where we want to go. But they also tether us to past experiences and learnt behaviours which can limit our view of ourselves and how we react to life.

We all have a repertoire of learnt behaviours. They are practised patterns of how we should react to pretty much everything that might come our way. They are behind the assumptions we jump to, in the defences we hide behind and, as I mentioned earlier, they are home to our suffering.

## Going Beyond Your Limitations

*Open your eyes, look within. Are you satisfied with the life you're living?*
– Bob Marley

A person bangs into you in the street. It hurts. As you are recovering you realise the person not only hasn't stopped to see if you are all right, they are already halfway down the street, seemingly oblivious to the fact that they nearly knocked you over. How do you react?

Is it proof that the world is full of inconsiderate people only interested in themselves? Are you outraged? Have they destroyed the good mood you were in and ruined your day? Or do you brush it off as obviously an accident and hope that the person makes it to whatever was causing them to be in such a rush? Or perhaps you feel embarrassed that you were not paying enough attention to see them coming?

Everything aside from the person actually bumping into you is an interpretation, including the strength of the bump. If you agreed with any of the above, your reaction is based on a belief you have formed over time about life.

Many of the limiting narratives we have about ourselves haven't changed since our childhood. This means that we are still living life according to our perspective of life as a child. As children, we were masters in creating coping mechanisms. We all have primal survival instincts and so, even as a child, we quickly deduced how to be and how not to be in order to remain safe. We learnt how certain scenarios played out and we acted accordingly. For example, if you grew up around someone with a quick temper, you learnt how to pre-empt an explosion, to run from confrontation so you didn't get caught in the firing line. We each created our own internal database of 'do's and 'don't's to stay safe. And voila! Conditioned behaviour was born.

A limiting belief isn't necessarily the result of something which actually happened to us or even something we witnessed. It can just as easily be formed by something someone told us – the rules and beliefs of our 'tribe' – or even a movie we've watched. It is our intellect trying to make sense of and pre-empt, or avoid, a situation happening, which it believes could be dangerous. It is our personal red alert system which tells us not to do X because we have proof it leads to something that is unsafe for us.

Whenever and by whomever they were formed, our beliefs and patterns all stem from a good place – our need to feel safe. The flip side of any learnt behaviour, however well meaning, is that it can put fear where none was there before. We can become scared to do something different to what seems like the 'norm' to us and we confine ourselves to the boundaries we made when we unconsciously decided certain things about how life is. The safety nets we or others put in place to protect us can end up strangling us and sentencing us to living life small. They actually prevent new and potentially wonderful experiences.

Just like the stories or 'life lessons' we have written for ourselves, our limiting beliefs are assumptions made about the business of life. They are not true. Really, they are a perfect example of the road to hell being paved with good intentions. They can rob us of vital life force and, worst of all, they can snuff out our dreams before they can even really form. We disregard these dreams as silly, unrealistic, not possible for people like us. We start getting in our own way. The harsh truth is that if we are not living the life we want, it is our own fault.

The good news is that it is never too late to change your story and change your life. It just needs a little courage to drop what you know and try life differently.

The quickest way to spot the limiting beliefs and patterns that are holding you back is to simply ask yourself which areas of your life aren't how you would like them to be. And how does the fact that they are not all you hoped them to be make you feel? Whatever emotion pops up in response, stay with it, because underneath that emotion probably lurks a limiting belief. If you feel a sense of hopelessness when you think about the glass ceiling you can't seem to break through at work, you may find that beneath the emotion is the belief that you are not good enough or perhaps yet again are being purposely overlooked. If you are someone who shies away from sharing your ideas in a meeting or with a group, it may come from being told as a child that you were silly or foolish and no one cared about what you thought.

Belief-busting involves following the emotional trail back to the original story. We know when we are on the right trail as the automatic defence system will immediately kick in. That's the cue for the string of excuses and the 'you don't understand' protest speech. It is the one in which you wholeheartedly believe that your situation is different and that there are real reasons why you can't 'because' or you can't 'until'. It can be used for anything from not asking somebody out because you are too old, young, fat, thin, etc., to not starting on the career path you dream of until you have another couple of degrees or courses under your belt. Most of us have experienced it – it is that moment which epitomises discomfort. Your friend makes a suggestion and your body, like a trapped rat, starts shifting around in your seat, your eyes dart everywhere searching for an escape and you desperately look for a way to change the subject. This is the moment when you have to decide whether you are going to put your energy into defending your belief or face your fear and accept that the belief is not only no longer working for you, it is actively blocking your potential, and let it go.

Once you have tracked down the belief intellectually, the most effective way to release yourself from it is to go to the energy around the belief. Remember: all our thoughts, beliefs and patterns are energy. So, notice what happens to your body when you think of the belief you want to release. What is the feeling like? Where do you feel it? Is it like a void in your stomach or a rock in your chest, does it zap you of energy or maybe feel constricting like a

clamp? A powerful way to release an energy is in ritual or ceremony. No, this doesn't mean you have to book a marching band
every time you want to shift some energy or get tribal with drums
and face paints. Rituals have been used throughout time to help
us to break through the wall of words and reach a part of us
which is more profound than the intellect, which tends to be binary.
Rituals are an expression of transformation. Think of the rituals
we still do – a bar mitzvah, a wedding, a funeral. Each one is
honouring a moment of transition.

The Shamans are masters of ritual. They understand the importance of a rite of passage, an initiation or an intention. These
become the highlights, the pivotal points in our personal adventure.
They are empowering memories of when we made a positive
change.

One of the oldest Shamanic practices is the fire ceremony. It is
used for different reasons, but here we are using it because fire
offers rapid transformation, to let go of everything we don't want
and call in all the things that we do. Traditionally, a fire ceremony
is done around a full or new moon to reinforce a moment of
change, but this is not essential. Nor is where you do it. If you
can, I recommend making a small fire outside somewhere in nature
(please be mindful) as it gives a sense of connection with something
greater than ourselves, but it can just as easily be done in your
living room using a small tea light. Work with what you have. You
will need some small twigs if you are doing it outside and some
matchsticks if you are indoors. It is the intention that is important,
not the size of the fire.

Give yourself time and space from anything or anyone who will
make you feel the need to rush or make you feel awkward. The

more you can allow yourself to settle into this ritual, the more powerful it will be. Enjoy it, embellish it, put your own heartfelt stamp on it.

## The three arrows fire ceremony

Depending on whether you are doing this inside or building a campfire outside you will need either three matchsticks or three twigs. They will be your three symbolic arrows: a Spirit Arrow, a Death Arrow and a Dream Arrow. Whenever we want to get rid of an energy which is bogging us down or holding us back, it is important to first acknowledge all the good things we have in our life.

Light your fire and sit still for a moment. Even if you are with a group, let it feel like it is just you and the fire. Then, when you are ready, pick up one of the sticks, this will be your Spirit Arrow. Using your breath, blow all the gratitude you feel into the stick. It is a conscious act of acknowledgement, a precious moment where you are saying thank you. This is not an itemised list, just one action which represents everything you are consciously or unconsciously thankful for. Then give it to the fire.

Sit still for a moment and then pick up the next stick. This is your Death Arrow. Bring to mind the limiting belief you want to let go of. Blow the pain and suffering you feel in your body into the stick. Again, it is the symbolic action of blowing, of letting go of all the feelings around the limiting belief, which can never quite be explained with words. By releasing the energy around the belief, we remove the hold it has over us. Give the stick all the heavy energy you feel and then give the stick to the fire. You are giving the energy to nature and shedding your limiting belief.

Once you've finished, again sit in stillness and then, when you are ready, pick up the final stick. This is your Dream Arrow. Blow in all your dreams of how you want to be – not what you want to do, but how you want to be in life – and give this stick to the fire. Imagine you are telling the world, the sun, the moon and the stars of your intention. By giving your dreams to the fire you are setting out your path. Be mindful when opening and closing your ritual. To make the place sacred you can open and close the ritual with a moment of silence or a prayer. There is no wrong or right way. It is up to you how you do it and how you make it meaningful.

## Which Part Do You Play?

*Once you label me, you negate me.*
– Søren Kierkegaard

If you were to stand up right now and introduce yourself, what are the four or five things you would say to give us an idea of who you are?

The chances are somewhere in the mix would be what you do and the roles in life that you play. The speed of life today demands that we get across who we are quickly. We live in an era where people want to know what our USP is – our unique selling point – even in our social life. Modern life favours a ready-made package to explain who we are and how we fit in, quickly and succinctly. None of us wants to hear someone's life story on a first meeting, we prefer a short trailer.

In today's world we place where people fit in by knowing what they do. We want to know our roles in life: son, daughter, parent, husband, wife, doctor, lawyer, artist, janitor, Shaman. Then we can label and box depending on whether we see the person as friend or foe, like-minded or a threat. For some it also gives an idea of our value and whether we are a person of interest. Most of us at some point in our life, possibly when dating, have been told we must meet 'so and so', they are a doctor, film star, rich, important. It is a prime example of how someone's role in life can supersede what kind of person they actually are.

We put people into groups depending on how we know them: work colleagues, family, new friends, old friends. Have you noticed how you behave differently with different people? We like to keep the different parts of our life separate. We are wary about anyone migrating from one group to another, because it becomes obvious that we behave differently with each one. When the groups become mixed, we are not sure how to behave. We don't know which role to adopt. Imagine sitting with your mother and your boss. Which character do you play – sweet son/daughter or the dynamic businessperson you are trying to show your boss that you are? It seems obvious that we are not going to behave in the same way when we are at work as when we are having a drink with friends. And, of course, we talk differently depending on whether we are speaking to a child, a police officer, negotiating with a car salesman or meeting the Queen. We all do it and it is perfectly natural. It is merely a matter of manners and showing respect to the person or the position they hold.

Unlike an actor, however, who knows their role is simply that – a role – and can leave it on set, we sometimes forget we are not the role. We actually become it and we carry the gravitas of the role into other areas of our life. We then start to worry how we will be judged if we come out of the role. Concerned that our behaviour will not be seen as becoming for a mother, business leader or police officer. And others may not make it easy for us to come out of role either, and so we can get trapped in being a character rather than ourselves. We have to be careful we don't become lost in the labels we use to identify ourselves. We need to be careful not to become attached to the role and behave accordingly or lose ourselves within it. Our roles in life are like the clothes we wear. They are not us. If we strip off all our roles, we still exist.

Here is a question to reflect on: How would you introduce yourself if you couldn't use any of your roles? Now who are you?

If we want to be truly free, we have to drop our ideas about who we think we are meant to be and remove all the labels and roles we dress ourselves in. We need to symbolically let go of them all. One way to do this is to write down each one on individual pieces of paper and burn them in a fire ceremony, or you can write them down as one long list and then tear the paper up into pieces. You can do this alone, but it is also powerful to do it with a group of friends. Help each other to see some of the unconscious roles we take on.

## The Story of You Reviewed

> *Become a mystery to yourself, not the sum of your past history.*
> – Alberto Villoldo

Without our limiting beliefs and the roles we play, the next piece to look at is the story we tell about ourselves.

We place great value in our life story. It is our way of telling the world who we think we are. Our story is a personal narrative made up of a collection of experiences we have carefully crafted to express and represent how we wish to be seen. We use our story to explain, excuse and defend. Sometimes we even use it as a weapon. We learn early on which parts hold an impact and which parts don't, and we adapt the emphasis of the story accordingly. Over the years our story gets pruned, embellished and polished through repetition to the point where we can tell it in our sleep. We are word-perfect – we even know exactly where we need to draw breath.

The story is so imprinted that we don't notice when it starts to become a fixed identity. We don't question our memories – why would we? They happened to us and we certainly won't accept someone else disputing them. We are highly protective of our story. We forget that it is a story full of cherry-picked experiences we have told ourselves and we forget that our story is just that, a story. It is version, not fact.

To really experience this and not just intellectually understand it, we can make it a self-enquiry meditation.

### 'Who am I?' self-enquiry meditation

Ask yourself: Who would you be without your story about yourself? Who is the 'I' having the thoughts? Stripped of everything you use to reference yourself against, what is left?

Before you sit down on your meditation cushion and set about answering this question, let me explain a bit about this style of meditation, because the first time I sat down to do a self-enquiry meditation I missed the point entirely. I was in Rishikesh in the

Himalayas sitting with a really kind young monk who had agreed to teach me a few different styles of meditation. In broken English he told me to sit comfortably, close my eyes and reflect on the question he gave me – the core spiritual question: 'Who am I?' So, I did, and every ten minutes or so I would open my eyes and give him an answer. Each time he would say no and bid me close my eyes again. This fed my competitive nature. It felt like a game and there I sat, even though my back was killing me, and racked my mind for the right answer. What I hadn't realised was that his English was not just broken but really limited, which meant he didn't have the words to tell me that finding an answer wasn't the point of the question. I got the message about an hour into it when he simply got up and walked off.

Spiritual questions are very different from scholastic ones. Rather than add to a store of knowledge about a subject, they are meant to dismantle you. So it is not about finding the right answer. It is not about copying someone else's experience. As you sit and ask the question 'Who am I?', it is hard initially to ignore your intellect scrabbling to find 'the answer', so start by going through who or what you are not. We are not our thoughts, we are more than our story. Let the question lead you beyond our thoughts, beyond our intellect.

Spiritual enquiry is used in many of the ancient spiritual traditions, in particular in Zen, which is famous for its koans. A koan can be a question, a riddle, dialogue or a story designed to exhaust the analytical mind. A spiritual question takes you beyond this analytical mind, to a place deep within you. As I discovered, no clever intellectual answer is required. In fact, it is best if you do not look for an answer at all but stay focused on the question itself. The question is boundless and, given time, it will open you up. An answer will confine you by instantly bringing you back to your analytical self.

We need to remember that we are more than any story we can create about ourselves. So, as the narrator, we can let our story open us to our potential. Our experiences may explain why we are the way we are, but it should be our choice whether or not they influence our future.

There is an old Indian saying, 'Use your memories but do not allow your memories to use you.' We are the storyteller and, as such, we can start to write a story which does not tether but gives us the freedom to fly, and to do what may seem to be the impossible: we can write a story which allows us to continue to evolve. Above all else, remember we are more than our story.

# Stepping Out of Your Shadow

## Shadowlands

*There is no sun without shadow, and it is essential to know
the night.*
– Albert Camus

We all have another story about who we are, but it is not one any
of us wants to tell. In fact, it is a story we do our utmost to keep
hidden, even from ourselves. A story we store deep down in our
unconscious. A story which holds our darkest secrets, a history of
our lies and everything about ourselves we have turned our back
on and would absolutely love to disown.

Welcome to the 'Shadow' and the 'Shadow Self', the part of
our psyche that has a big impact on our everyday lives and yet
most people don't even know of its existence. The Swiss psychologist Carl Jung, who coined the term, defined our Shadow Self as
'the person we would rather not be'.

It is a storehouse for all of the feelings and impulses we have
rejected because we were told, or decided ourselves, that they were
ugly and unacceptable. It is also home to our inner judge and jury,

the chattering voices that keep a record of our flaws and failings and see it as their duty to keep us in check.

You might think that it is probably best to leave your Shadow Self well alone. What's the point in opening a potential can of worms? Leave things be. However, before you decide to completely disassociate from this part of your psyche and your less attractive character traits, know that the Shadow is also the storehouse for some of our greatest attributes. Which means it is also the proverbial bushel under which we hide our light.

The roots of our Shadow Self are planted in the 'don't be' world of our childhoods: 'Don't be greedy/mean/selfish/loud/a smarty pants/a show-off' . . . you can delete as appropriate. Our Shadow Self was made when our childlike excitement was shot down and we were told not to make a scene, not to brag or get too big for our boots, and we were swiftly put back in our place.

This is not about blame, but knowing that our then yet-to-be-fully-formed inner moral compass at times jammed, as we went about learning the rules of how to behave and how to 'fit'. It is hard to know why one rebuke or look made an impact and the rest didn't, suffice to say though that we can all remember moments in our past which were humiliating and made us feel small, stupid and unlovable.

The problem is that while we might want to reject all the qualities we don't like, it doesn't quite work that way – by simply turning our back on them, it doesn't mean they miraculously evaporate. They simply continue to direct our lives like the wizard behind the curtain.

Try as we might to repress these aspects of ourselves, it doesn't stop them finding a way to remind us they are there. The more we push them down, the more likely they are to spring back and slap us in the face, often like a Freudian slip at the most inopportune moment. So, we learn to fear our less endearing emotions and feelings, such as anger, impatience or jealousy, as well as our natural talents which make us stand out from the crowd, like a brilliant mind, for fear they will bring unwanted attention. We swallow our temper and pretend to ourselves and everyone else that we are an easy-going, laid-back person, only to go and completely lose it over something tiny. Or we stop trying to excel because we learn that being overly competitive is unattractive and not a fast track to popularity.

The Shadow Self is also known as our dark side, but it is not our Mr Hyde to our Dr Jekyll, and, what is more, there is nothing evil about it. Ignorant, yes, in the sense that it needs to learn to handle our not-so-sweet self, but it is certainly not something we need to be scared of. In the same way as a Ferrari or a racehorse is not dangerous, only more sensitive and complex, our Shadow Self needs handling with care. This is because it is visceral and the feelings which it is made up of are raw and unhealed.

The Shadow is not simply an intellectual concept. It is better thought of as a quagmire of intense and untamed emotions which we hold in our cellular memory. Everything in it has an energetic charge, so our Shadow will often create unpleasant physical responses. In short, our body expresses what our mind represses. We might not understand why we are physically reacting, but nonetheless we do. The Shadow is behind all those times when we have reacted way, way, way out of proportion – the instant irritation, the rage which causes our blood to boil, disdain which makes our nose scrunch or the disgust which makes our skin crawl. Embarrassment which makes us want the ground to open up and swallow us, the compliment which makes us want to squirm, or the adulation we spurn because we just don't know how to handle it. It is responsible for those inappropriate knee-jerk reactions which don't feel like a conscious response or even that they are under our control. Emotions which, just with a thought, make you want to physically cringe or curl up and die.

The thirteenth-century Sufi spiritual master and poet Rumi had an amazing ability to capture the complexities of simply being human. His poems reaffirm that nothing we struggle with today is new and that our ancestors also held the same confusions and fears and had to work through the same range of feelings. This is a poem I often ask clients to read, because it shows us that, rather than fearing so called negative emotions, we can choose to befriend them, all of them. It shows us that they all act as helpful signals, highlighting where we need to focus our attention.

*The Guest House*
by Jalaluddin Rumi (translated by Coleman Barks)

> *This being human is a guest house.*
> *Every morning a new arrival.*
>
> *A joy, a depression, a meanness,*
> *some momentary awareness comes*
> *as an unexpected visitor.*

*Welcome and entertain them all!*
*Even if they're a crowd of sorrows,*
*who violently sweep your house*
*empty of its furniture,*
*still, treat each guest honourably.*
*He may be clearing you out*
*for some new delight.*

*The dark thought, the shame, the malice,*
*meet them at the door laughing,*
*and invite them in.*

*Be grateful for whoever comes,*
*because each has been sent*
*as a guide from beyond.*

## Being in the Know

**Hello darkness my old friend, I've come to talk with you**
**again.**
– 'The Sound of Silence', Simon & Garfunkel

One of the biggest fears in life for a lot of people is the unknown, so it is a little crazy so many know so little about themselves. We wonder about what others are thinking – debating and dissecting their actions – and yet we don't question what's really behind our own thinking or behaviour. Once we have recognised that we, too, have a Shadow Self, we can explore it and start to understand what lies behind some of our less comfortable emotions. Just like the cellar losing its spookiness the moment you turn on the light, the same applies to our darker emotions. They are not the same as digital trolls – as soon as we bring them out of hiding, we can appreciate their purpose.

Once out in the open, its adverse effects dissolve. This is important, because if we don't recognise them and own them, they will own us. Unaired and unaddressed they are capable of causing deep ongoing suffering and fuelling harmful habits. They are the source of self-hatred. Whereas by reclaiming our flaws and our formidableness, we get the chance to stand in our power. The ancient Greeks understood this. They personified the human emotions in their gods and goddesses. Ignoring any of them, regardless of whether they represented a supposedly light or dark emotion, was done at your peril.

The myths show how they were all capable, if slighted, of making your life hell. The ancient Greeks understood that any part we disown within us turns against us. They understood that the human soul is a paradox. Just like the Greek gods and goddesses, we too can behave with virtue or venom. We all have the ability to behave from one extreme to the other.

This is why we like the anti-hero in a movie or are fascinated by the unpredictability of the villain. They represent a part of us we can't normally tap into. As a teenager most of us admired the rule breaker and thought the rebel with or without a cause was cool. It was our way of exploring a part of us we were pressured to silence. It is a natural part of our development and so it is important to realise that we are not in battle with our Shadow; it is not something we need to conquer or eradicate. It is something we need to understand and integrate because only then can we feel whole.

Human experience is full of paradoxes, it is made up of contrast. We like to see things as either/or. We see duality in everything. We have an idea of good and bad, pleasure and pain, light and dark. But this idea suggests that there are parts of us that we are OK with and parts of us that we aren't. It reinforces that there is a right way to do something and a wrong way. There are good people and bad people. Terrorist or freedom fighter. It allows for judgement, and with judgement, of course, comes blame. It separates us into an 'us' and 'them'. In the main, most of us want to be seen as a good person doing the right thing, living life the right way, hence why we do our best to repress our less saccharine emotions. We want those around us to see our good side and what we consider to be our great qualities. But we need to understand that the duality we see in the outside world is actually mirroring our inner world.

We cannot appreciate good if we don't understand what it is to be evil. As Jung said, 'To the degree to which we can condemn others and find evil in others, you are to the same degree unconscious of the same thing in yourself or at least the potentiality of it.' We all have the potential for kindness, thoughtfulness and loving; we also all have the potential to be selfish, cold, even cruel. It is important to see that the Shadow and the Shadow Self aren't the bad to our better self. Just like yin and yang are interdependent and form a oneness, the Shadow Self is an essential part of us.

We have to own that we are all capable of the same violence, war and brutality which we abhor. When we stop beating ourselves up and become a little gentler with our foibles, we stop being so acutely aware of and reacting to everyone else's shortcomings. The same goes for judgement. When we can accept that we, too, have shortcomings and love the fact we stay just as we are or choose to make changes, we have more compassion for other people and theirs.

The term may be new, but Shadow work features in every blueprint for personal development and transformation. Everyone on a spiritual path or wanting to become a psychotherapist has to face their Shadow Self. It is one of the keys to knowing yourself; a crucial point on the road to enlightenment.

Every spiritual master has had to face their demons. Jesus met the devil in his forty days and nights in the wilderness; the Buddha was tormented by Mara while sitting under the bodhi tree. Holy men and women, yogis and Shamans continue to isolate themselves in hermitages, caves and the rainforest in their bid to befriend their demons. Getting to know your Shadow is an essential part of healing and becoming whole. It brings with it relief and an enduring inner peace. You stop getting spun out by bizarre mood swings and blinded by emotion, and start being able to see behind the feeling. You accept that every aspect of us, just like the ancient Greek gods and goddesses, has a need to be heard and, if we give it a voice, it is less likely to take us by surprise or harm us.

An emotion is like a messenger – it signals an underlying feeling that needs our attention. It shows us that a part of us is being stifled and needs to be addressed. If you have anger issues and lose your temper over the smallest thing, it simply means you get overwhelmed and cannot cope with the rush of energy. You get consumed in the moment and so it comes out as a rage, a spiteful comment, a tsunami of tears. We hit out with words or, worse, physically in a bid to escape and offload the pain we are feeling. Watch a little toddler when they get overwhelmed.

They have a very simple coping mechanism, which is basically to have a complete meltdown. The only way they can regain balance and release the excess energy is by having either a tantrum or hysterics. Job done. They can then go back to playing. But in a mere matter of years we all learn that there is a third option where we don't have to deal with our feelings at all, and we start storing away everything we can't cope with – and so the Shadow is born.

When we start to read the signals properly, we realise that all our emotions are simply doing is giving us a heads-up, a friendly advantage.

## It Takes One to Know One

*Love your enemies, for they tell you your faults.*
– Benjamin Franklin

A traveller walking from one village to the next stops to chat with a monk sitting under a tree by the side of the road.

'I'm on my way to stay in the village ahead, do you know what it's like?'

The monk looks up at the traveller and asks, 'Where have you come from?'

The traveller says, 'I have just come from the little village on the other side of the hill.'

'Ah, how did you find it?' the monk asks.

'It was awful,' the traveller sighs. 'I was meant to stay a few days, but to be honest I didn't like the village. The villagers were so cold, unhelpful and rude, I couldn't wait to get away.'

'Hmm, you'll find that the village ahead is much the same,' responds the monk.

A while later another traveller comes across the monk still sitting under a tree by the side of the road. On seeing the monk, the traveller stops and asks, 'Excuse me, can you tell me what the village ahead is like?'

The monk looks at the traveller and asks, 'Where have you come from?'

'I have just spent a couple of days in the village on the other side of the hill.'

'Ah, how did you find it?' the monk asks.

'I loved it,' the traveller replies. 'The village was sweet, the people were great, they really made me feel at home.'

'Hmm, you'll find that the village ahead is much the same,' responds the monk.

How and what we see in the world is merely a reflection of our own inner world. The upside to this knowledge is that we can use the world around us like a mirror to see the bits of ourselves we wouldn't otherwise know are there. This is particularly true when it comes to our Shadow Self, because not only is it well hidden, deep in our unconscious, but if its existence feels in any way threatened, its defence walls spring up. Should anyone suggest we are projecting our own negative traits, we can put our hands on our heart and flatly deny its existence.

But we all cast our own Shadow onto everyone around us: friends, family, colleagues, those in our community and those in the public eye. Be assured that as you internally judge another for being bitchy, jealous, selfish, pathetic, stupid, this is your Shadow in action. Here is the rub. The simple truth is that we can't be sparked by something in someone else if that something doesn't exist in us as well. Every single quality we can recognise in another, lives in us as well. Of course, we can intellectually understand a plethora of personality traits, many of which may not be active in us, but we are highly unlikely to be triggered by one we have no experience of. So, although you may not own the trait in the same way, if you get a physical reaction, take it as a cue that it is time to do some Shadow work.

Argue as much as you want, whether it is: 'I am not mean/a liar/unkind/bitchy/aggressive/greedy/ruthless' or 'I am not talented/ beautiful/cool/popular/special'. If it sparked a reaction in you, it exists in you. Here is a really irritating observation: when you point your finger at someone else, there are three fingers pointing back at you.

The strength of your aversion to a particular trait in someone else simply highlights the strength of your rejection of that same trait in you. We get sparked by people who display the same aspects we have disowned. We don't like it and we get irritated. The aspects we despise or love in someone else are mere reflections of our own qualities. When you see someone else daring to be selfish, greedy, gloomy or any trait you haven't made peace with, you will struggle to let it pass without comment. But if you are by nature a little greedy and you know it and have stopped beating yourself up over it, it won't bother you when you see greed in someone else. It's not about condoning or not condoning it, it just won't get under your skin. But if your greed is an emotion that you have suppressed, either because you have decided or been told it is a bad thing to be, you will definitely have a reaction when you see it in someone else. Below is a good exercise for catching some of those traits.

## How to spot your projections

Think of a person in your day-to-day life who you find highly irritating; somebody who never fails to annoy you. Who is the first person who springs to mind? Take a moment to think about what it is about them which makes them someone you can't resist criticising or do your level best to avoid. Which characteristics wind you up the most? Is the person needy, obtuse, short-tempered, mean, smug, gossipy, a know-all, competitive or controlling? There is no guessing required; if you have picked the right person you will have more than one thing which gets to you. We physically feel the characteristics we abhor like an electrical charge. Yes, whatever it is that makes them insufferable is a projection of the same suppressed character trait sitting in your Shadow waiting to be recognised and heard.

But just as we can project our Shadow, so we can also project our light. Again, when you find yourself pointing at someone and thinking they are an inspiring, wonderful, kind, compassionate person, there are three fingers pointing back at you. What you are seeing in that person is your own hidden light. We can only see in others what we have within ourselves. Think about someone you admire, perhaps someone for whom you have feelings of awe. What is the primary quality or attribute you most admire in this person? Maybe it is their courage, their conviction, their charisma, their intelligence, their creativity, their talent. What's the quality you admire most? Look for how you display the same qualities in your life.

If you struggle with either of these exercises you can always do them with a friend or, if you are really brave, resilient or plain insane, someone in your family – they will have absolutely no problems getting straight to your Achilles heel.

When you find a trait or attribute which you can own, sit with it. This is not an excuse to berate yourself, so try not to judge. Track back through your life to see where it comes from, when you first disowned it. Flashes of anger may come from swallowing it when you were little. You know if it has worked or is on the way to working as the next time the trigger will either have gone completely or it will be a lot less full-on.

## Self-sorcery

*Nothing makes us so lonely as our secrets.*
– Paul Tournier

There is a powerful sorcerer in all of us – the dirty look which hits or the little comment fuelled by jealousy planted purposely to open a nugget of doubt in someone else. We can all do it, but more potent than any black magic spell a voodoo doctor can cast is the sorcery we do to ourselves. Everything that makes up our Shadow Self depends on secrecy and staying behind the scenes to simply survive.

Along with being a home to the bitch/bastard in us, the Shadow is also a breeding ground for guilt, shame and our innermost fears. The darkness the Shadow provides is a haven for the ultimate weapons of self-sorcery, like guilt and shame, to thrive.

Each of these has a particular and easily recognisable physical feeling: the cold sweat of fear that wakes up the body with a sharp electric shock running through the brain; the heavy burden of guilt which feels like the weight of the world on your shoulders; the isolating warm flush of shame that floods through the body.

Unaddressed guilt and shame are two of the strongest forms of self-sorcery. They can be all-consuming and like a slow torture as they both eat us from the inside out. Guilt is the feeling we get when we have or believe we have done something bad – it sits on our conscience. Shame is the feeling that we are bad and unlovable because there is something fundamental and deeply wrong with us. Both are crippling emotions which fuel self-hate and a feeling of being 'lesser than' and 'unworthy'. When they are allowed to grow out of control they act less as a moral compass and more like a wrecking ball, obliterating our world and tearing us away from any sense of connection with others, including our loved ones.

There is nothing to be achieved in letting self-hatred fester. It is possibly one of the few times when 'time' harms rather than heals. An immediate and effective cure for many is talking. The Catholic Church is not alone in advocating confession; many of the traditions, from Tibetan Buddhism to modern psychotherapy, all understand the power of talking. 'Shame', for one, cannot survive in the limelight; it depends on you keeping it a dark secret.

## Press Pause

> *Between the stimulus and the response there is a space. In that space is our power to choose our response. In our response lies our growth and our freedom.*
> – Viktor Frankl

Rather than allowing these negative emotions such as shame or guilt to isolate us, we need to actively create a distance from them; to press the pause button on the internal dialogue. In exactly the same way as you might pause a song or a TV programme, you can pause your thoughts. Because our thoughts become habitual, half the time we don't even notice we have toxic thoughts running in the background. When we press pause and step away from the noise and question the internal feedback, we can start to reclaim control. As Eleanor Roosevelt said, 'No one can make you feel inferior without your consent.' That includes us. When we are consumed with the shame of who we are or what we might have done, the pause can give us just enough time to remember we do not have to be a slave to our thoughts. We have a choice.

However, it will mean absolutely nothing to be accepted by others if we don't learn to accept ourselves. A meditation I like to do is a variation of the Buddhist 'maitri' practice. Maitri, also known as metta, is the first of the 'four immeasurables', which describe the four qualities of love. Maitri is a Sanskrit word which can be translated as 'loving kindness', but to truly be able to feel it, we first need to forge an unconditional friendship with ourselves. As the Buddhist nun Pema Chödrön explains, maitri is being able to relax with yourself, being able to feel at home with your own mind and your own body. It is the basis of compassion, a sense of well-being and of being glad to be alive. Traditionally you start with bestowing love and kindness on yourself and then extending it out to family, friends and everyone in the world including all sentient all sentient beings. It is like the airplane safety procedures where you put your own mask on first before helping others. You can find an authentic version of the maitri meditation with Pema Chödrön online.

Making friends with ourselves can't come from the outside world. It has to start from us. We can know our friends and family might love us deeply, but it won't touch our sides if we cannot learn to be kind to ourselves. However, although we all have seeds of love within us, conjuring up love for yourself is really hard if you struggle with self-hate. So, I also teach it the wrong way around as a prequel to the traditional meditation – see below.

Remember there is a reason why it is called a meditation 'practice' and not meditation 'nailed it first time' or meditation 'done and dusted'. If you want to run a marathon you will need to practise, and meditation is no different. Just as a run (allegedly) can vary one day to the next, so does a meditation practice.

## A love and kindness meditation

Read through the following and then give it a go. There are no fixed rules – be playful with it, make it work for you.

- Sit on a meditation cushion, a chair or a sofa. Sit upright if you can, but be comfortable, do not exaggerate a forced straight back. If you sit correctly over your sit bones, the spine will naturally do its job without any muscular effort. Close your eyes and have the sense of a warm smile washing over you.
- Bring your awareness to your breath and your body breathing. Be in this moment, doing nothing other than enjoying riding each wave of breath like a surfer on the ocean. Let the eyes soften, feel the smile in your eyes, the corners of your mouth, in your heart.

- Now, in your mind's eye, see something or someone straight in front of you who you love, unconditionally, with all your heart, with your whole being. This is your anchor image – it can be a pet, a person or even the young innocent you. Let it be something or someone you love so much that just looking at them and imagining them in front of you fills your heart and body full of love.

- As the love builds, start extending it out to other loved ones. Keep extending it out; you can include those you love but don't know, you can include spiritual teachers like Jesus, Muhammad and the Buddha. Keep extending your love to all sentient beings – extend it to everyone.

- Now let this feeling of love you have for everyone include you too. Open heart, loving eyes, kind mind. Feel the same healing flow of love you extended out to others flowing through you too. As you imagine everyone and everything you are sending unconditional love to, notice in their eyes the same love you are bestowing on to them being directed towards you.

- If you find it hard to visualise, simply think of those you love and then extend it out repeating in your mind, 'May you be filled with loving kindness'. Extend it out to everyone you know and then to all sentient beings and then hear them repeating it back to you. If you struggle to accept the love from others and/or yourself, just notice it. It's a practice – like the runner, the more you do it the easier it will become.

## The Energy Mandala

> *The secret to life is meaningless unless you discover it yourself.*
> – W. Somerset Maugham

Variations of energy mandalas have been used throughout history to alter energy. Tibetan monks make sand mandalas as an intricate focus of meditation and to purify the energy. Native American Shamans in North America create unique sand paintings for a person to lie on top of during their healing. This particular energy mandala is an ancient Shamanic practice which I often turn to. Talking is a powerful tool, but there are times when you can feel all talked out or that you are caught in a loop, or just no words can quite describe exactly what it is you are feeling and, even if they can, they do nothing to help you shift them.

We get caught in telling the same stories over and over again, polishing them into works of art, instead of finding a way to let them go. Creating an energy mandala is a dynamic process. It is an act of transformation. It is also a meditation, a powerful moment when you can step out of time and access a profound part of you beyond the wall of words, beyond the noise of the intellect. This energy mandala is an opportunity to release the energy caught in your Shadow. It is a symbolic painting ideally using items from nature, but there are no rules, so if you are housebound, use items from around your home. It is extraordinarily powerful at transforming the energy around a situation or a deep mental wound in your personal life. But they are all, one way or another, made for healing. When someone first explained to me how to make one, I was pretty dismissive. I can remember thinking it all sounded a bit arts and craftsy. Only when I was actually persuaded to do one, and not just intellectually understand its benefits, did I see quite how powerful they are. Like all Shamanic practices, understanding can only come from experience.

Energy mandalas are a symbolic painting expressing the energy behind a feeling or emotion that you would like to process. They are excellent at helping you get out of your head, to pause, to sit with the emotion without looking to intellectually solve it. Because more often than not, intellectually understanding why we feel something doesn't actually do anything to help us stop feeling it. Fears, feelings and emotions don't always make sense. It should feel like you are giving a deeper aspect of yourself, which exists beyond your intellect, a voice. Energy mandalas are a highly effective way of transforming the energy around a situation or feelings around a person – the pressure on your chest, the empty feeling in your stomach or constriction around your throat as if your voice is being silenced. What I love about them is their ability to help resolve and find peace without words. They have a magical quality.

Before you begin, set an intention for the mandala to help you make peace with the energy around a feeling, a situation or a relationship. Use the advantage that everything that makes up our Shadow Self has an energy charge. There is no need to bring it to the level of the intellect and express it in thoughts, the shift can all happen at the level of energy. Concentrate on the visceral feeling, the energy you actually feel in your body. What happens in your body? Is it like an electric shock, a sick feeling in your stomach or a heavy weight on your chest? Does it feel like it courses through your veins, blinds you or makes you feel ungrounded? Your language here is energy not poetic words, so you don't need to worry about how you would describe it to somebody else. This is particular and personal to you.

If you can, make the mandala outside. This is by no means essential, but there is something wonderful in allowing nature to energetically get involved as well. My one recommendation is to allow yourself lots of time and privacy. You might not need it, but this is for you so why rush it? See the following simply as a guideline. There is absolutely no wrong way to do this, avoid questioning yourself. Use your imagination and be creative. Follow your instincts.

## Creating an energy mandala

Before beginning your mandala, collect items from nature, preferably from the ground – leaves, flower petals, stones, debris, anything that you like the look of or that feels right. Make a circular frame with some twigs. If you are making your mandala indoors, use small objects from around your home that feel right. You can draw the frame, or alternatively you can bring nature inside.

Using everything you have collected, make an abstract picture depicting the feelings you have around the emotion you are working with. If, for example, you want to make peace with feelings of shame, first allow yourself to feel it, let it come up. Now, as if you had no words, how can you, like an artist, represent the feeling in the mandala? Place the items inside your circle in a pattern that speaks to you. Don't think about it; simply allow your unconscious mind to direct what you pick, and how you arrange and rearrange your items.

When it feels right, sit with it. This is your energetic portrayal of the emotional wound in you. When you are ready, ask yourself: What do I need to do to the picture to change the energy, to transform it, to heal the wound and find peace? Move the items around; this might involve removing some and adding new ones. Again, follow your instincts. You can keep the mandala for a few days so it can be a work-in-progress which you keep coming back to. When you do a mandala outside in the open, nature might well decide to join in. If the wind picks up and blows parts of your mandala around or away, be happy. You are getting a helping hand from nature. When it feels like it's finished, let the mandala speak to you, notice the emotions and insights that come to you. Once you feel you have finished, dismantle it, dispersing the items back to nature.

# Walking to Your Own Drumbeat

## Do You Remember Who You Really Are?

*Wisdom tells me I am nothing. Love tells me I am everything.*
*And between the two my life flows.*

– Nisargadatta Maharaj

This step is about waking up to all the different ways that we behave which smother rather than enhance our originality; the things we do which take us out of our true self so that we might be accepted, approved, and keep us from evolving and embracing our uniqueness. All of us want to fit in, somewhere. It is the tribal instinct I mentioned earlier, and the best way to do this is to make sure people like us. It means that sometimes we go along with the pack, even when we don't want to, just to keep the peace and fit in. We don't want to be the one to rock the boat in case we get chucked out of it. The question is, to what extent are you prepared to go?

Versatility is a valuable skill and being able to adapt and dance to someone else's drumbeat can be fun. It gives us both choice and an insight into other ways of doing life. However, when we continually allow it to drown out the sound of our own drumbeat, we can lose a sense of ourselves. It is essential to keep our drumbeat within earshot, so when we veer too far off our own path, we can always find our way home.

The reason we ignore our own needs is that we want to be loved and accepted by others, and we can often assume that others know better. We do our best to stifle the little nugget of growing resentment, even though all it is doing is simply trying to signal that we need to regroup and recentre. It is our own red alert warning system that we are in danger of losing a sense of what is true to us. In short, there is nothing wrong with pack mentality so long as we keep a sense of who we are within it.

It is so easy to find yourself going along with a collective dream without even questioning it. Advertising agencies depend on it and most of us have drawers of never-used gadgets to prove it. They tell us what to dream for and what will make us happy and fulfilled. But have you ever stopped to question whether the ideal you have about what a perfect life is, is even yours? Did you consciously choose your dream, or have you inherited it or adopted the popular ideas of the moment? The more we look to the outside world to tell us what will or won't actually make us happy, we are in effect disregarding our own take on life, not wanting to be the odd one out. It stops us tapping into our own uniqueness.

Developing our Spiritual Intelligence does not necessarily mean we need to make sweeping changes to how we do life, becoming a lone wolf amongst the sheep, adopting a 'my way or the highway' approach. It is definitely not about denying yourself the fun things in life. It is about getting a better understanding of yourself and noticing how you get lost or disconnected or self-sabotage.

Awareness gives us choice, and it puts the responsibility for how we go about life firmly in our hands. Knowing who we really are beneath our stack of behaviours gives us a strong foundation and allows us to be nimble-footed and quickly regain our footing when we get knocked by life.

## The question of you

Here are some questions to mull over. An answer may spring to mind immediately, but don't worry if one doesn't. The power is in what the question opens up and where it leads you. Maybe put the book down and allow yourself a moment to wonder. It is a moment to focus on yourself in the same way you might look at someone else.

- What in your eyes makes you unique? What are your quirks which make you, you?
- What are your special qualities that other people see in you? How do they describe you?

## Changing Faces

*Will the real Slim Shady please stand up?*
   – 'The Real Slim Shady', Eminem

The novelist Gabriel García Márquez said, 'All human beings have three lives: public, private, and secret.'

If our 'story' is a selection of snapshots from our private life and our 'Shadow' is the shelter for our secret life, then our 'persona' is our public performance. The persona is our idea of how we think we need to come across in order to survive and thrive. It is a cultivated image of how we want to be perceived by the outside world. It is our personal marketing machine where we get to practise our poses and ensure the world catches our best angle. Back through the centuries when people spoke Latin, the persona was the name for the different theatrical masks that actors would wear on stage. Today in psychology, again thanks to Carl Jung, it's used to explain the public faces we all have. In many respects, we are really no different to the masked actors of old as we masquerade through life. We wear different masks for different people, and few, if anyone, get to see the 'true you' behind the facade. William Shakespeare nailed it when he said, 'All the world's a stage, And all the men and women merely players.' A prime example of exaggerated personas is the Versailles 'court' manners. Think of the duplicitous nature of the characters in *Les Liaisons Dangereuses*.

As with everything, some wear their masks more gracefully than others. There are those who, like a chameleon, can switch effortlessly. Their facades are sophisticated and seamless, and it is hard to know if they are actually wearing a mask at all. Then there are those who hide behind a very formal and official two-dimensional mask, who are like shut books and it is impossible to gauge who the real person is behind it, or even if there is one. Then there are others who wear such ill-fitting masks that the facade fails to hide their true feelings, and everyone can see the two faces at the same time.

We learn the value of personas and how to use them as children. They help us fit in, but, much more importantly, they help us to protect our fears, feelings and fragile egos. If you think about it, quite a lot of social education as a child is learning how to hide our true feelings. We learn how to put on a brave face, keep a stiff upper lip, put on an act of not caring and smile when inside we might be falling apart. In short, it is part of all our early life education to learn how to lie to the world, making out we are one thing when we really feel another.

At school, the smart ones cotton on quickly to the benefits of a persona. Appearing strong and thereby getting to keep their lunch money. Becoming the joker in the class to fit in, or the all-rounder who gets on with everybody. We adopt a persona we believe will bring us love and acceptance. A persona which persuades the world we just don't care, or to look elsewhere and that there is nothing to see over here. We become the comedian, the charmer, the confidante, the 'too cool for school', the quiet one, the fashionista, the rebel, the wit, the bitch, the bastard, the bully. We behave a certain way to get into our chosen clique as a child, or club when we are older. And just like the stage actor, we use a number of props to sell our persona, from the right trainers, haircut or clothes to, as an adult, the type of house we live in, the car we drive or where we go on holiday. We know that everything we do says something about us, and we can manipulate it accordingly.

Some of our persona is down to society's demands and how we expect each other to behave. There are times when we all have to behave contrary to how we feel, for example, making polite conversation with a grown-up when you were a child pretending you were interested when really you wanted to be somewhere else (actually, that never changes). Of course, it's simply social intelligence that we need to behave differently in different situations, and we use different personas to be able to do that.

Our personas, per se, are neither good nor bad, but it is really important for our well-being to be able to distinguish our masks from the 'us' that stands behind them. Because when we lose touch with the 'us' behind the mask, we are losing touch with our core sense of self, and when we lose touch with that, it can make us feel both lost and empty; like a flickering hologram vying for existence.

When we become more concerned about how other people see us or think about us than our own feelings, we are basically putting not just our happiness but our mental well-being in other people's hands. And it is only a matter of time then before we are afraid to be ourselves or say how we truly feel. In short, personas aren't bad until they become fixed, or they become more developed than the person behind them.

A world-famous celebrity is obviously going to behave differently when they are in front of the cameras to when they are hanging out at home with their family and friends. They have a carefully crafted brand to sell and they need to maintain an image. If they are unprepared for the pressures of fame, however golden the pedestal the public put them on can fast become a prison and uproot them. The heady heights of stardom become a nightmare as they find themselves feeling like they are free-falling, flailing in space, isolated, lost and removed from any sense of reality. We see it time and time again with public meltdowns as personalities grapple with the unexpected mental suffering the dream life brings, and they try to remember who they really are and reclaim it from the grips of their image.

Thanks to social media, this problem is no longer exclusive to those in show business, but stretches from the influencer stuck in their bedroom to the middle-aged mum posting on Instagram.

Massive popularity and fame is now achievable without ever having to leave home, and with it come its problems. As the persona gets edited in an attempt to maintain popularity, the focus becomes more on who we think we should be and trying to predict what people want.

Some of the effects of social media simply magnify what happens when we forget ourselves in favour of our public image. It highlights our insecurities and whether, deep down, we feel a nobody without our masks. Although our personas might seem like they are our best bit, just as a beautiful rose head cannot survive without its stem and roots, nor can we. The thrill of being a somebody is addictive, and then finding new ways to maintain our popularity and saleability is fuel for anxiety and depression.

But we don't need to fear stardom. If we have strong roots, a strong sense of self which comes from the detox, and become aware of what's what, we have all the foundations we need to fall back on if and when we lose our footing.

## Looking at your mask collection

It's hard to see our own masks, not just because they rarely come in the form of the exotic feather formation you might see at Rio Carnival, but also because we are wearing them. A simple way to work out what yours are is to see how your behaviour differs between different situations. Take a moment to think about the ways you behave in order to be liked, to fit in with people, including your friends and family. Are you always the diplomat? How often do you find yourself begrudging that, yet again, you are doing something you don't particularly want to do? What stops you from just saying no?

As you go about your day, start to notice when you are not being natural or honest. Who are the people you really feel comfortable with? The ones you can completely relax and be yourself with without any judgement?

Remember a time in your life when you felt unjudged and relaxed just being you. Close your eyes and remember what it felt like as if you are there right in this moment. Notice how you hold your body when you feel this way; notice what happens to your mind. Does it feel busy or calm? Notice the speed of your thoughts, or have they disappeared? Do you feel like you are caught in the past or the future or do you feel present? Really take a moment to enjoy the sensation – let it wash through every cell of your being so you can remember it and come back to it whenever you wish.

## Perfection is Flawed

*Always live up to your standards – by lowering them, if necessary.*

– Mignon McLaughlin

We are living in the era of the airbrush. Anything less than perfect can be instantly erased. Like human topiary, we prune and preen to perfection. We edit and airbrush in an attempt to portray to the other airbrushed images that we, too, are winners in life. It is a universal lie that we are all involved in, and yet we can't help but continue to compare our lives to the other fabrications and then, unsurprisingly, find ourselves wanting. Perfection is a destination we think we will reach where we will finally be able to stop striving, relax and enjoy everything life has to offer. But anytime we think we have finally reached it, we realise it is like one of those mirages in the desert, a capricious illusion. Perfection is nothing more than an unfulfilling abstract concept which is completely subjective. We all gauge it differently – the perfect partner, perfect looks, perfect holiday, perfect life.

Striving for perfection is very different from the pursuit of excellence. Perfection is a finite, it leaves no room for error, whereas excellence is infinite and often grows out of our mistakes. In Taoism, perfection is considered akin to death as, by definition, it is a goal achieved, job done, the end. There is no more growth, no movement either way, and so no life. Food for thought indeed!

Deep down, we all know that there is really no such thing as perfection, but we need to keep it as an unattainable ideal we can strive for, always just out of reach, the carrot to our donkey. Perfection feeds our insatiable appetite for more, it leaves us never being satisfied with things as they are or by how we are. Perfection is a belief that we shouldn't rest on our laurels, there is better around the corner, that we are never good enough, that we can always be better, physically, mentally, spiritually. Perfection is a bar set high, a promise that when you reach the goal you will have a better everything.

We create 'should-do' lists, generic lists of things we think we need to do if we want to be a better, happier, more perfect person: get fitter, eat healthier, practise yoga daily, meditate twice daily. And when, within the month, the 'should-do' list for happiness gets buried under the just-delivered case of wine, we feel a failure. Oh, and we also project this on to others, not just those in the limelight, but our partners and sometimes even our children. We become disappointed and disillusioned when they don't do things the way we think they 'should be' done or fail to live up to our high expectations, and prove themselves, like us, less than perfect.

This is not a matter of dropping your goals, it is about understanding that reaching them does not mean your whole life, in a genie in the lamp puff of smoke moment, will suddenly be transformed. Losing those five kilos may well change your appearance, but you won't necessarily lose your problems and you will still be you. Pause for a moment and ask yourself what exactly are the goals you are striving for and what do you hope to happen when you achieve them.

It is ironic that the Japanese culture, which on the surface seems to demand perfection from its people, is actually the birthplace of two art forms which revere imperfection. Wabi-sabi is an ancient philosophy that grew from Zen, which embraces the beauty of not just the imperfect but also the incomplete. It allows everything to be as it is, and everyone to be as they are. Perfect because of the flaws, not despite them. Just as in nature we accept that everything is in a state of process and we can see beauty in all the four seasons, each stage of life is also perfect as it is and does not need to be changed. It is the perfect (sorry) antidote for the pressure of constantly trying to improve everything. It embraces the natural character of things, the unfinished, the dents of time, the storylines engraved in a face. Kintsugi is another Japanese art form which celebrates imperfection. Broken pottery is put back together, but instead of trying to hide the breaks and make the joins invisible, the pieces are joined using liquid gold, drawing your attention to the breaks. It is creating a work of art which celebrates the unique flaws and embraces the imperfection.

Our ideas of perfection keep a hold over us because we never really take a good look at them or question what we actually mean when we talk about something being 'perfect'. Let alone the small point of how you can be certain that your idea of perfect *is* perfect.

A young monk in charge of minding a small garden in a Zen temple was told by his abbot that some important guests were arriving later that afternoon. The young monk, proud of the garden, wanted to make sure it looked its best for the guests, so he immediately set about making it perfect. He painstakingly pulled up all the weeds, pruned any untidy tree branches, trimmed all the shrubs and combed the moss. As he was meticulously raking the carpet of autumn leaves and gathering them up, he noticed an old Zen master sitting watching him intently from the temple. After several hours of dedicated hard work, the garden looked pristine; it had been a true labour of love.

The young monk looked over to the old Zen master and with a sense of pride called out, 'What do you think, the garden looks perfect now, no?'

'Hmm,' the old master answered as he looked at the young monk's work, 'but there is something wrong, it is not quite right, let me help you.'

The old Zen master got up and slowly walked up to the tree that stood in the middle of the garden. He looked at the garden for a moment and then, grabbing the lower branches, shook the tree with a strength that belied his age so that all the colourful leaves started to shower down all over the garden.

'Now it is back to perfect!' the master smiled at the young monk as he slowly walked away.

## Copycat Copycat

*Most people are other people. Their thoughts are someone else's opinions, their lives a mimicry, their passions a quotation.*

– Oscar Wilde

I can remember when I was little, I would say whatever my big brother said. I basically did my level best to be his carbon copy. I copied him in just about everything. If he liked chocolate, I liked chocolate. If he didn't like chocolate, then I (begrudgingly) also didn't like chocolate, and if he (way ahead of me) in the very next breath changed his mind, so did I, of course trying to make it look natural and simply a coincidence that we both felt the same way. When the inevitable 'stop copying me' would come along, I would protest my innocence, an argument would ensue and then the tears would come. Probably not dissimilar to a lot of people's childhood; older siblings, around the world, getting frustrated and infuriated by their younger siblings hell-bent on riding on the coat-tails of their individuality.

Following in someone else's footsteps can certainly open up our world to new things, but it can also stop us from developing our own voice. It is worth remembering that Christ was not a Christian, nor the Buddha a Buddhist. Jung even went so far as to exclaim, 'Thank God I am Jung and not a Jungian.' What they have in common is that they all bushwhacked their own path using their own life experiences. When we try to walk along another's path we are always going to be slightly off balance, it is a little like trying to literally walk in someone else's footprints on a sandy beach. The reason it is tricky is because we are moving to somebody else's natural rhythm, and however fantastic it is, it is not ours. We will always feel a little uncomfortable and awkward as we have to check not just that we are doing it right and according to the book, but we also have to constantly try to pre-empt their next step. Not all of us want to carve out our own path – you could argue why bother if someone else has made a perfectly good one we can use. It's a fair point. However, when we just follow what someone else has done or said, we do not draw the answers from within us. It's a little like being a passenger in a car; you don't need to pay attention to where you are going, someone is doing it for you. Which is fine, until you get lost. When we don't have a deep understanding, we have to hold on too tightly and there is no room for any movement. There is no lightness of touch. We are rigid and clumpy.

We are also looking for someone else to supply us with a method of being. Our focus is always somewhere out there. We stop listening to our own thoughts, our own rhythm and allowing our own style to develop. We never learn to trust our own intuition. What's more, however well we emulate someone else we will always fall short, because it doesn't come from us so we will always feel like we are just a little behind the beat, reinforcing the idea of 'I am not good enough', of being a fraud or imposter syndrome. We can only feel truly safe when we move to our own drumbeat.

If you want anything to have any authentic substance, you have to draw it from your own experience. Your life needs to be your expression; that way it can grow and evolve. It is one of the things I particularly love about the Shamans and medicine men I trained with. They didn't really say much; their method of teaching was giving you the experience through practice. It was very much hands-on. Once they felt comfortable that you knew what you were doing and understood the work, they encouraged you to find your own way within a safe framework. Each one of them approached the work slightly differently. It had nothing to do with wanting everyone to be an individual, just that when you copy you can't put your heart into it, you can't truly connect to what you are doing, it will always lack feeling.

## Rusty Halos

*The impression that you are a demigod worried me. I wanted to be like an ordinary human being with virtues and vices.*
– Nelson Mandela

For a lot of people, the whole purpose of being spiritual is seeking to become perfect or, put another way, 'spiritually enlightened'. Really, nothing could be more perfect. But it is a heavy goal which tends to curb life rather than enhance it. It brings with it the mother of all should-do lists, which we feel must be adhered to if we are to have any chance of obtaining it. Spiritual enlightenment has become an ideal, a high bar made from hearsay and assumptions that if you continue to focus on it, you are guaranteed to always fall short. The yogi, one minute with head bowed and hands in prayer position 'at one with the universe' oozing wisdom and serenity as they chant 'Om', are five minutes later swearing at the traffic as they rush to get to their next appointment, not an ounce of serenity left. We can't maintain our perfect selves for more than a few perfect moments, and so instead of allowing our spiritual practice to flow through all our life, it gets compartmentalised. We have our spiritual life and then our real life, and never the twain shall meet. My advice is to put down the list and call off the search. The more you try to be spiritual, the more removed you become from yourself. If you have to be something which is different to how you truly feel, it is theatre. Life will show you everything you need to know about yourself if you let it, and quieten down enough to hear it.

Spirituality comes with expectations from yourself and others. There is an idea that if you follow any form of spiritual tradition, or indeed are a qualified psychologist, you must have transcended all mental turmoil. Because if you haven't, you are plainly not very good at what you do. So, the humbleness goes out the window as again the airbrushed images try to prove to each other how spiritual they are, hoping no one will realise that they don't actually meditate every day, as though that were a mortal sin.

The spiritual world, like every other world, has its fair share of carefully crafted personas. Gurus seemingly waft through life like floating divine beings with wise expressions receiving the accolades from unquestioning devotees hanging on their every word. They give the impression they have transcended mere mortalhood – enlightened beings free of human flaws and failings – reaffirming that you are 'lesser than', with an awfully long road ahead of you.

We have to be careful of making someone else a demigod. Devotion is a lazy form of living. We need to take responsibility for ourselves and our actions. This also means that when that person does something to disappoint you, which they invariably will, you will not find yourself floundering in free-fall. Unless we are prepared to have our own experiences, we will always have to bow to other people's perceptions of how we need to be and what we need to do.

There is an ancient Zen koan by Linji which says, 'If you meet the Buddha on the road, kill him.' When we spend our life listening to great gurus and teachers explaining life, we can stop actually living it. They can become the biggest distraction from doing your own work. Linji is basically saying we need to find our own Buddha nature, and we cannot do that if we focus on how we think our experience is meant to be according to another, rather than on how our experience actually is right now and work with that. The joy of everyday life is that it will continually offer up your stuff to you. Unless you run off to that mountain cave, life, like an ever-vigilant teacher, will show you where your work is. Whether it is the burst of irritation you feel when you find yourself behind a line of faffers when you are in a rush, or a spark of envy at someone else's success, it is in these moments that our spiritual mask of benign knowing and serenity goes out the window and we know we have work to do.

I can remember early in my training telling my mentor, when he asked how I was finding the training, that as much as I loved it and wanted to believe everything I was learning, I couldn't shake off the sceptic in me. He looked at me with a stern face and told me never to stop being a sceptic. He said Shamanism was not about blind belief, it was about experience; to listen to what others said with an openness and interest, but believe nothing until I had had the experience myself. Then you don't have to believe, you will know.

His Holiness the Dalai Lama must be at the top of the pile when it comes to spiritual teachers. He is, after all, considered to be the fourteenth reincarnation of Avalokiteshvara or Chenrezig, the bodhisattva of compassion and the patron saint of Tibet. Yet he sees himself as a simple monk, with human flaws and failings, just like me and you.

He makes a point of telling stories about his own shortcomings. In one I particularly like, he is laughing throughout as he tells of a time as a young man when he became jealous of one of his officials who had a better relationship with one particular bird in his aviary than he did. He would watch as this pretty little parrot would let the official stroke its head as it ate seeds from his hand. His Holiness wanted the bird to display the same love for him, but the bird wouldn't let him go anywhere near him. Put out by this as he was, after all, His Holiness the Dalai Lama, which surely meant the bird should love him more, he decided to take on the official's duties for a few days and feed the bird himself. He wanted to prove it was just a matter of spending some time with the bird. But, try as he might, the bird showed no interest in complying with his wishes. He lost his temper and told the bird off, destroying any future possibility of a friendship between the two of them.

## Dancing to Your Own Drumbeat

*Where's your will to be weird?*
— Jim Morrison

Dancing to your own drumbeat doesn't mean having to be contrary; it simply means making sure you include yourself, your thoughts and your feelings in whatever you do. It is taking ownership of your uniqueness and the fact that you are not the same and you won't always fit in or want to. It is choosing to develop your own style rather than going along with the fashion. Bizarrely, one of the hardest things any of us can do is 'just be yourself'. Possibly because if we want to be our authentic natural self, it means we have to address all our insecurities and the biggest obstacle of all: our fear.

Fear comes in many guises . . . Fear of not being liked or accepted. Fear of making a fool of ourselves. Fear of feeling vulnerable. Fear of failing. Fear of stepping into our own power and our own potential. Possibly the biggest fear of all is the fear of being seen – seen for everything we are, flaws and all. The only way any of us can feel comfortable in our own skin and experience true freedom is when we stop hiding the bits of us we decided along the line were unacceptable. That means allowing ourselves to be vulnerable. For the Shamans, when you stand up and let yourself be seen without trying to hide anything about yourself, then you stand in your true power.

Take a moment and ask yourself: What are three things that I have been afraid of all my life? Put the book down and have a think about it. What are the first things that spring to mind? Maybe write them down. Now ask yourself: What are three things I haven't done in life because of my fears? Are you OK with this or is it perhaps time to face the fears which continue to prevent you from living life the way you would like to? Take one of your fears and give it your full attention, see exactly what it is supposedly protecting you from. You may well find you are being stopped by a childhood fear which you have already outgrown.

# Outside of Time

## The Great Wake Up

*Vision is the art of seeing what is invisible to others.*

– Jonathan Swift

If you have ever wondered why all spiritual gurus – Maharishi Mahesh Yogi and Master Shifu in *Kung Fu Panda* alike – have the same bemused all-knowing look about them, it is simply because they can see that the world is an illusion and that life is little different to the dreams we have at night. When spiritual traditions say the world is like an illusion, they are not saying the world doesn't exist. The world exists, as does all the material stuff around us. Anyone who has attempted to walk through a wall will be able to verify this.

When they say the world is an illusion, they mean it is deceptive in its appearance, not that it is a puff of smoke disappearance act. They are referring to the surface world of objects – all the things with which we identify ourselves and our self-worth, like our houses, cars, jobs and belongings which represent our thoughts, opinions and beliefs. The material world would like us to believe that it is the be-all and end-all and the only thing which matters.

But it is only a matter of time before it comes up short and we start to question if it is perhaps just a sideshow.

You don't need to be a great guru or a mystic to wake up to the realisation that the world is an illusion. It doesn't have to happen in a lightning flash like a magician's big reveal. Many people, regardless of whether they consider themselves spiritual or not, know that life is a dream, they just might not term it that way. For most of us, waking up from the dream state isn't a one-time event. It is more of a penny-drop moment on repeat. Seeing through the illusions of life comes and goes, a little bit like glimpsing blue sky behind passing clouds – a moment of being enlightened and then being pulled straight back into the illusion by yet another attention-grabbing drama. That said, the realisation is an experience you can't unknow, so although we may continue to get fooled and sucked in, we do get better at quickly recognising what matters and what doesn't.

The ancient yogis refer to this realisation as opening the 'third eye' (Ajna). Our third eye is our sixth sense – it gives us a clarity of vision that extends way beyond what our eyes can physically see. When our third eye is open, we get to relish life's twists and turns in the surface material world we all play in, without being drawn in and tripped up. The twists and turns can no longer hurt us, because we can see how the world is made up of a collective illusion, a dream we are all co-creating together, which we then call reality. Using the steps laid down by the spiritual masters of the past, we can find our way through the illusion once and for all. First, however, we have to understand the nature of our thoughts and witness how they behave. Only then can we get to see exactly what it is that lies beyond them.

## Thought Bubbles

*I was dreaming I was awake and then I woke up and found myself asleep.*

– Stan Laurel

One way to look at the world is as a collective concept – a cocktail of thoughts, ideas and principles which pop up and then disappear like bubbles in a glass. When we wake up to the fact that it is our thoughts that create our world, the old adage 'change your thoughts and you change your life' seems like an obvious move to take. However, as with most adages bandied about, it is often far easier said than done and the question remains: How? Sadly, it isn't simply a matter of reciting a list of positive affirmations into the bathroom mirror each morning and then sitting back waiting for your life to magically transform. These may help, but really you are just topping the cocktail with some garnish.

To make a lasting change in our lives we have to get to grips with how our thoughts actually behave. For this, it is less about what is on our mind and all about the space our thoughts take up in our mind, and the different ways in which they monopolise our attention and stop us being present in our own lives.

When you stop and consciously pay attention to each of your thoughts, you may notice that they are neither particularly interesting nor original. Most of the thoughts we are having today are exactly the same ones we had yesterday, they simply loop around and around like the same old dishes on a conveyor belt at a sushi restaurant enticing you to choose them. Just as it is not obligatory to pick up each dish as it passes by, nor do we have to engage with each and every thought that vies for our attention, particularly if it is one we don't like.

The problem is that we don't always get the pleasure of picking which thought to have. It can often happen the other way around. One minute we are happily eating sushi and then, in the next, our thoughts have taken us off into a virtual world of wondering or worrying about something that either has happened or might never happen. All that is left in front of the sushi is our body alone. Does it matter? In short, yes. Because this is at the root of many mental illnesses. When we let our mind continually split off and isolate itself in its own world of thoughts, after a while we start to lose the sense of being in our body and feeling grounded. It feels like we have literally disassociated and that we are floating above ourselves or somewhere far away. The more time we spend lost in thought, the more isolated we become from the world around us. We feel cut off from a fundamental sense of connection, and this can lead to anxiety and depression. When this happens, and it does happen for all of us, we need to have a way back – a sense of connection – and the quickest way is through our senses. It is hard to look after your mental well-being if your mind and body are never in the same place at the same time.

To reconnect, do the five senses meditation laid out on page 22. What can you see, hear, smell, taste, and how does your body feel? It takes only a minute, so it is a perfect exercise to do each and every time you realise you have got caught up in your thoughts, even if that is fifty times a day. It is especially important as the simple fact is our thoughts have complete control over our health. Our thoughts have the ability to empower or disempower us, with the latter tending to shout the loudest. The truth is it doesn't really matter how our life changes on the surface, our thoughts control our state of mind and it is that which dictates whether our palace is a prison or our prison a palace. More important than what our thoughts tell us, is how our thoughts affect us and where our next thought will send us and why.

There is a little Zen story about a man sitting by the roadside who suddenly sees a rider come flying out of nowhere, galloping towards him like a madman.

The man cries out to the rider, 'Where are you going in such a hurry?'

'I don't know,' the rider yells back, 'ask the horse!'

The agility and versatility of our thoughts is extraordinary. They can behave like time machines propelling us years back into the past or spinning us off into the future. Anyone who has ever struggled with trauma will know from experience that thoughts pay absolutely no attention to the linear time kept by the clock on our watches or smartphones. They also show complete disregard for the rule that states that time is a straight line running from the past into the future. Triggered by one thought, a person can find themselves back at the traumatic event which may have happened years ago, living it in real time. Conversely, a quick whiff of some homemade chocolate brownies and you can find yourself transported straight back to your childhood waiting for your mother to take them out of the oven, or a song which takes you back to your first kiss. This is the dream state.

Thoughts also have the power to be physically palpable, cranking up our sensory levels to acute. In a blink they can make our heart race, make us feel sick to our stomach, reduce us to a bag of nerves or leave us in a pool of sweat. We may ask ourselves how anything which isn't real can physically affect us, but just like the monster in a nightmare, our thoughts are part of the dream state. They seem very real right up until the point when we wake up.

Thoughts can be so absorbing that they can disconnect us from not only our bodies, but also our own surroundings. We become unconscious of the bird singing outside or the conversation going on around us. Thoughts can even keep us from the moments we look forward to. Have you ever found yourself sitting having dinner with one of your closest friends to find the only conversation you are really listening to is the one going on in your head? Body and mind split into two different locations. This too is the dream state.

One thing all our thoughts have in common is that they keep us from this moment, this one right now. So, it is not surprising when we end up questioning what happened to our life or wondering where the day or even years have gone, when for so much of it, we weren't actually there. Our thoughts are the dream state.

It may seem that thoughts get a tough rap, the scapegoat in spirituality, always being singled out as the bad guys and blamed for all our suffering. But this isn't an anti-thinking campaign on behalf of 'Zombies Inc.' or a swipe at the very thing behind human evolvement. Life without our ability to analyse, process, dream and create is not worth thinking about. But as important as our ability to think, is our capability for awareness. Spirituality does not advocate being devoid of thoughts, just to realise that there is more beyond them. It is simply a shift in position, so thought follows awareness. Our being at the beck and call of our thoughts is really as ludicrous as the sheep herding the sheep dog.

## New Friendships

*Don't walk behind me; I may not lead. Don't walk in front*
*of me; I may not follow. Just walk beside me and be my*
*friend.*

– Albert Camus

Mindfulness is an extremely effective way to get our body and mind in the same place at the same time for any length of time. A recent study showed that our mind wanders 47 per cent of the time. This means that for nearly half our lives we are not actually here. Instead of living life, we spend our time either lost reminiscing about the past, thinking about the future or consumed with thinking about this, that or the other.

In theory nothing could be simpler than mindfulness as all you have to do is be here now. But it is the staying here which proves to be a little tricky, because our minds enjoy going off on walk-about. Staying in the present moment, without letting your mind drift off, is surprisingly difficult even when you consciously try.

Try it for yourself:

- Put the book down and, when you are ready, close your eyes and bring your awareness to your breath.
- Notice your inhale, the air going up your nose, down your throat and filling your lungs and belly.
- Hold the breath for a couple of seconds and then feel your exhale of air leaving your belly, lungs and out through your nose.
- As you exhale, have the feeling of letting go, relaxing.

See if you can do this twenty times without getting distracted by a thought.

Your mind is mighty and majestic. It is wilful and it likes to run free. A good way to imagine it is as a magnificent and powerful wild horse, running where it wants, when it wants, darting left and then right, watching and reacting to even the slightest movement or change in its environment. Treated kindly and gently, you can not only tame your mind but forge a priceless friendship – a loyal ally in life, ready to help rather than hinder. This is why meditation is part of every single spiritual and religious practice, because it is in meditation that we really get to know our mind. Meditation is normally found in the 'you know it's probably good for you but not exactly fun' pile. But there is no reason why meditation has to feel like some arduous back-breaking chore. True, to reap the benefits you do have to show up, but like all great friendships, the more time you spend with your mind, the stronger the bond becomes. Our mind only runs aimlessly around, like the wild horse, because we haven't given it any direction and it doesn't know us. If you want to befriend your mind, just like with a wild horse, it needs time for a trust to grow. Only then will it feel safe enough to relax and cease being continually spooked by its own shadow. It is a matter of gently coaxing and cajoling and constantly turning up, and little by little it will start to stay with you, each time a little bit longer.

The purpose of meditation is not to control your mind by using heroic levels of willpower, but to befriend it, and every time it does go darting off, to calmly call it back. When you learn to meditate you are told not to try to stop thinking, but when a thought runs away with you, as soon as you realise it has taken you off, just to bring your awareness back to your breath or whatever the focus of your meditation is. It is a little ironic that we need to stop and remember to be mindful, but we do. A pocket of time carved out for us to be present in the present. Even though sitting on a cushion at an allotted time can be a sanctuary, a chance to press pause amid the chaos of a day, it's not always possible.

Chan and Zen Buddhist monks and nuns see mindfulness as much more than just another type of meditation practice. For them it is a way of being and something we can all do throughout the day, whatever we are doing. As with everything in spirituality, the whole point of doing it at all is to make you feel better and to hold you when life gets tough. So, if you are thinking, 'Crikey, I can cope with twenty minutes, but to maintain a meditation marathon which lasts the whole day is a little too hardcore', please trust me. It is not, and it will help with any mental turmoil you may have. It involves staying connected with your inner state and, when you notice that your mind has gone walkabout from whatever it is you are doing (which it will, continuously), simply calling it back, in the same way you would if you were doing a formal meditation. Try it for yourself. Today or tomorrow, go about your day exactly as you would, same pace, do nothing differently except, when you drink your coffee, taste it, savour it. When you have your shower think about nothing other than the act of having a shower. Feel the water, the temperature, without letting your thoughts run to what you need to do next. It might not be so exotic, but you have just as much chance of attaining enlightenment while washing the dinner dishes as you do while meditating in the lotus position on a Himalayan hilltop.

# Watching Cloud Shapes in the Sky

*When you change the way you look at things, the things you look at change.*

– Albert Einstein

The more you practise mindfulness, the more you can enforce some social distancing from your more toxic thoughts. You can become the witness of them rather than the victim to them. Being able to step back and observe rather than always being in the thick of it is particularly helpful for anyone struggling with trauma and overwhelm. This witness state sees our unprocessed painful pile of emotions and feelings from arms length. When we become the witness, it gives us some breathing space and a chance to get a better perspective. It is a valuable skill in everyday life, as it cuts down the number of knee-jerk reactions. It gives us a little more space to watch the thought or emotion arrive without immediately being hooked in by it and swept along by our own reactions to those emotions.

Being the witness is an effortless state – it is like lying on a beach watching the waves coming in, without the need to judge each wave on how well it did compared to the one before. As the witness we can go about our day without feeling obliged to react to anything in it at all. Again, this is not a call for wannabe zombies; reacting is very different to responding.

Being the witness to our thoughts is leaning on the fence watching our friendly wild horse playing in the field. Watching it graze, run around and just be a horse without an opinion or the feeling that you need to jump in and start running around chasing it in a bid to catch it and bring it under control. Letting it be, just the way it is. When we witness our thoughts, we realise that we are not our thoughts. We can't be, because if we were, we wouldn't be able to watch them. So, we are not one and the same. By separating ourselves from our thoughts we reclaim control of how they flow through our mind. If we are not our thoughts then we are not the anxiety they bring either; we are not the depression, nor are we any of the things our thoughts are telling us we are.

If you are someone who struggles with mental anguish, this is a powerful and effective technique and worth practising. The more space you can create between you and any unpleasant thoughts, the easier it is to duck and dodge them when they try to knock you down. It is also wonderfully relaxing not having to comment on absolutely everything as it passes or to feel obliged to entertain it – like the guest who overstays their welcome. A silent observer watching your thoughts without attachment or comment. Fundamentally, it is understanding that a thought has no importance until we give it an importance.

## Silent witness meditation

This is a relaxing meditation. It is one of my personal favourites, particularly as I have a mind which can fill up quickly with thoughts and opinions. This is my turn-to when my internal judge gets a little too loud and starts ad-libbing on the mic. It helps me to reconnect with the inner stillness we all have, which in turn means my nearest and dearest can come out from under cover.

The art of this meditation is just to sit and do 'no-thing'. It is not about trying to achieve a special state or, for that matter, achieve anything. You can do the meditation either inside or outside. Either way, the theme of just letting everything be as it is remains the same. If you can do it outside or by an open window, do it with your eyes open and allow nature in. Use all your senses to engage with everything around you, without feeling the need to interpret or add anything. To just be present with what is, hear all the different sounds – birdsong, cars, planes, voices and other people's music – merged together into a symphony of sounds. Actively recognising things as they are, even if they are not exactly how you would normally like them to be. Hear it all without opinion.

If you do the meditation indoors, make sure you are sitting somewhere that is really comfortable. There's no need to sit like an apprentice monk – allow yourself to relax – and there's no need either for others to have to tiptoe around you. If you find it is easier to focus on your internal world when your eyes are shut, that is fine. If you would like to try the meditation with your eyes open, that is fine too. You have probably now got the gist – do it as you do it, no rules.

- Become aware of your breath. Notice that you are breathing and how each breath is different. Don't try to change it or formulate it, everything is perfect just the way it is. Notice how some are deep, some shallow, some wide, some thin. Notice how your body is breathing just fine without your input. Everything is perfect just as it is. There is nothing to do, nothing to change, let everything be just as it is.

- Witness how your body feels when you just let it be. Scan your body, letting yourself become aware of each part as your scan passes it. Witness your chest rise and fall just like an ocean wave, notice the temperature on your skin.

- Now bring your attention to your mood. Witness your feelings. Don't try to change them, just listen to them. There is nothing for you to do but be a silent witness.

- Watch your thoughts as they pop up and dissolve. However much they try to entice you, just let them be; there is no need to engage with them – let them pass like a bird flying in the sky.

- Watch yourself watching yourself. Be the watcher. Let go of the you who is meditating. The part of you who might be trying to meditate well, who might be trying to get it right. Let go of the part of you trying to change or to make something happen. Everything is perfect just the way it is. There is absolutely nothing for you to do but watch and relax.

- Watch the watcher. That is the one giving the continuous commentary and grading your performance in life. Watch it as it tries to hook you, and be aware that when it doesn't succeed, it may well change tack and start complimenting you on your progress. So, when your internal voice exclaims, 'Wow, well done, look at you sitting there letting everything be just as it is; you've mastered this, you are probably ready to do more advanced meditations now,' or 'I wonder if I look spiritual and as at one with the world as I feel', ignore it.

- Your thoughts will keep finding ways to distract you. Witness that too. Like being the fly on the wall of your mind without reacting to anything in it at all, when we stop trying to control, a space opens in us. Let the space be a natural, effortless state of awareness. This is our baseline before it becomes covered with thoughts. We are all naturally fully aware. We are not the thoughts which bobble along the surface. It is an inner calm. It is an ocean of peace. Relish the effortlessness. It is the core of who we are. Relish the quiet.

- When you are ready, become aware of your body and your body breathing. Take a few deep breaths and then, when you are ready, open your eyes.

This meditation can take you into a deep state of relaxation, so once you have finished, it is best not to pilot a plane straight away or hit the clubs. Give yourself some space to let your senses settle.

## Empty Cups

*Sell your cleverness and buy bewilderment.*

– Rumi

There is a famous Zen story of a university professor who visits a Zen meditation master. As they sit down for tea, the professor starts to talk about the concepts behind Zen and meditation. As the professor talks on and on, the Zen master quietly pours the tea. He pours the professor's cup right up to the brim, and then keeps pouring. The professor watches the tea overflowing everywhere until he can't contain himself any longer.

'What are you doing? The cup is already full, you are wasting the tea,' he exclaims to the master.

The Zen master replies, 'Your mind is also full, there is no room for anything more. Until you empty your mind, anything I say will also be wasted.'

The art of 'no mind' (mushin) is at the heart of the Zen

practice. No mind is being able to empty your mind and let go of what you think you know about everything, so you can always be ready to see life from a fresh perspective. Whereas the expert's mind is closed, a beginner's mind is open and curious. The famous Korean Zen master, Seungsahn, used to call it 'don't know' mind. It is an antidote to an apathetic attitude of a 'Been there, done that, got the T-shirt' mind, which drains the zest, colour and magic out of life. It is one of the most powerful practices of all because when our mind is already stuffed with a pile of preconceived ideas, we close down life, we make it finite. A finished book. It fuels boredom and same-same fever. It creates a dissatisfaction with life which eats away at our spirit. Life becomes hell in paradise as nothing can impress us, as our tastes grow increasingly particular and we constantly look for the new and the better to interest and entertain ourselves. We forget that, as anyone who has faced death knows, the wonder and joys of life are found in simple things, simple moments and simple actions. Keeping beginner's mind alive in us gives us boundless energy and zest for life. Most important of all, it keeps the child in us alive.

Our intellectual self likes to place things, box them up, label and tick them off. Like a curator of the museum of life, we put a label on absolutely everything. It is, after all, how we are taught from the 'get go' and there is no denying it, it's an effective way of getting to know what's what. The bird singing in the tree exists regardless of us being able to identify it or label it. But as soon as we hang a label on it, we diminish it and we desensitise the magic of a bird singing in a tree. We lose touch with the miracle of life: flower, sky, ocean, bird, tree. Because we can name them, we think we know what they are. But unlike when we saw them for the first time, we no longer see the marvel of what we are looking at. A tree is just another tree; a bird singing is just a bird. As we label, we consciously clock it and then immediately dismiss it – we lose the wonder and the magic of what it is we are looking at. It is not that we are tired of being awestruck, touched deeply – we travel the world looking to be spellbound by a new wonder we haven't seen before or thrilled by a new experience – we simply need to realise that, when we look with fresh eyes, we can see every day all around us how extraordinary and magnificent our world is. With beginner's mind we can see the bird singing in the tree every morning and be awestruck at the wonder of life. What do you see, hear, smell, taste, touch and feel when you look at the world without labels?

Beginner's mind is acknowledging that each and every moment is a new moment. Nothing remains the same. We miss out on the delights when we take anything for granted. Just as we can't cross the same river twice, we have never been in this moment before. Each moment is brand new. Each moment is always fresh, always unique. Whatever you are doing today or tomorrow, don't take the backpack of past experiences, ideas and opinions with you. Go empty-handed and try looking at everything and everyone with fresh eyes. See how it feels to be free of all your preconceived baggage and to see things anew. Notice how those around you respond when they are not being judged or diminished into a box. It brings an openness and spaciousness to things and to our relationships, letting everyone and everything have the room it needs to stretch and to grow.

The Shamans I trained with in the Andes all have a wonderful childlike quality about them; an innocence and sweetness. Their simple lives mean they have dodged the cynicism of the modern world and know how to embrace life. They never seem to tire of what for them are common occurrences. Walk with them in the mountains and they will stop in awe, not just at the magnificence of the condor flying high above them, but at the view they have seen thousands of times before. I can remember when I first noticed that they seemed to be mumbling something quietly as we walked. When I asked one of them what they were saying, he told me he was saying thank you. Thank you to the mountain, the bird in the sky, thank you to Pachamama (Mother Earth) for looking after him. They took nothing for granted, seeing everything and everyone as special. Simple folk living lives rich with wonder. I always wear one of their white beaded bracelets which they make in their spare time to sell. It acts as an anchor for me. Each time I notice it throughout my day, it acts as a reminder not to waste my day caught up in thought, and to look around and be grateful for the joys which can only really be found with a beginner's mind.

## Right Here, Right Now

*To live is the rarest thing in the world. Most people exist, that is all.*
– Oscar Wilde

Mindfulness is all about embracing the present moment, because only when we are here in the 'Now' are we actually in touch with life. Ironically, mindfulness, contrary to its name, is about emptying the mind. That said, it is actually a heart practice. In Asia the word for mind and heart are the same. Mindfulness has been around for thousands of years and is a perfect example of how these ancient spiritual practices have stood the test of time. It is a discipline which helps us to reconnect with everything and everyone, including ourselves, so we can experience life fully. It is basically a love affair with life.

In mindfulness you learn to recognise that this moment is the only moment that actually exists. Everything, including the past and future, can only exist in this moment, which actually isn't a moment, because a moment is a measure of time and the present is a timeless, continuous 'Now' with no beginning or end.

In short, there only is 'Now'.

When we are fully here in the 'the Now', we stop projecting ourselves out of ourselves and so become less vulnerable to our minds taking a free rein and running away with us. As someone who often gets consumed by thinking, I find that the power of mindfulness is in the fact that when I land back in the Now, my thoughts do not come with me, they can't. Because when we are fully focused in the moment, there is no room for either our thoughts or the incessant chattering voices. We come back into our body, which is obviously always in the Now. This makes it not just a haven for anyone who struggles with mental anguish, but if you continue to practise, a real escape from mental turmoil. By definition, if there is no place for our thoughts, excluding when we purposely choose to focus on one, it means any painful thoughts cannot survive while we are in the Now. It's like having your foot on the home base in a game of tag – you can't be touched. Look down at your hand. As you look at your hand, notice if even only for a hair's breadth your mind went quiet. In that hair's breadth you found a sanctuary, a stillness.

An extreme example of truly being in the Now without any background noise whatsoever is being in a life-or-death situation. Imagine walking down a narrow path in a rainforest and coming face to face with a hissing snake. Be assured that not only will you come to an abrupt standstill, so will your mind. It will return from wherever it was in an instant. Any thoughts you might have been having a nanosecond before – be it daydreaming, making plans for tomorrow or lost in a painful thought or emotion – will disappear. You won't see them for dust. Even your internal judge, bar some initial expletives, will put a sock in it and maybe for once be helpful. You will experience an alert, cold, sharp awareness as you focus your complete attention on the snake.

Adopting a mindfulness practice gives you the ability to tap into that moment when your mind goes quiet in your everyday life, without having to endure an exhausting or terrifying adrenaline rush. If you can experience that stillness even for a hair's breadth, you have found an answer to how to quieten your own mind anytime you wish. It means you have the gap between thoughts, where you can help yourself with depression, fear, anxiety, stress and shame. It means you have the ability to reclaim your mind from the toxic thoughts, emotions and fears that you thought would always stalk you. A hair's breadth where you touch an inner peace and have a moment's respite from the internal noise is a start, a gap which can steadily increase.

The easiest way to come back to our senses is through the breath – the bridge which links our mind and our body. If your mind has taken you anywhere you don't want to be, bring your attention back to your breath. If you bring your complete focus to your in-breath, the thoughts will disappear. For as long as you can stay in the Now, you are free. Sometimes our mind is so frenetic it makes focusing even on the breath hard. When this happens, it helps having something to say, but it needs to be something pretty innocuous and bland. So, as you inhale, say quietly to yourself, 'I am breathing in' and, as you exhale, 'I am breathing out'.

At Plum Village, the French retreat centre founded by the Vietnamese Zen master Thich Nhat Hanh, the monastery bell rings every fifteen minutes. At the sound of the bell, everybody stops whatever they are doing, whether it is cooking or contemplating, so they can come back into the Now. They bring their awareness back to the in-breath for at least three breaths and then they go back to whatever it was they were doing. This effectively cuts the hypnotic trance most of us fall into as we go about our day. Don't worry if you don't have a big monastery bell or Tibetan bowl to hand – the timer on your phone will do just fine. It is a simple exercise which only takes a few seconds, but it is effective because it keeps our mind on a long puppy-training lead so it can never run away from us for too long.

The act of showing up 100 per cent to whatever we are doing and being present in our own experience is not simply for our own mind management, it is also a priceless gift we can offer another person. Giving someone your full attention is letting the other person know that you see them. At the beginning of any relationship we are pretty good at this, mainly because we want to be there, so we are properly present. Then, as we get to know the person and they perhaps become a part of our lives, we see them, we hear them, but we don't necessarily *listen* to them. We hear the words, but not what is behind them. This can happen between partners; it can happen between parents and their kids; and, of course, vice versa. It becomes a bad habit and one that makes nobody happy. There in body, but not in spirit. Being too busy to be present for others also means we are not there for ourselves.

If you want to give mindfulness a go, it doesn't mean you have to make dramatic changes to your life – it simply means becoming more aware. You don't have to approach the rest of your life at a solemn snail's pace, palms touching in front of your heart as you mono-task with a demure deliberation. Nor is it about kicking back and hoping that the universe will sort out your life for you. We all need to make plans. It is part of life, and there are times when we need to pick up the pace. Instead, you can see mindfulness as a valuable skill that you can use at anytime, anywhere, when life for whatever reason gets too overwhelming.

Mindfulness is a holistic practice which enhances all aspects of our lives. The science is out there. It helps us come out of the automated trance-like existence of doing things simply out of habit, with little thought, or, for that matter, pleasure – whether that is continuously shopping or wolfing down our food. Anyone who has ever fasted or done a detox knows how delicious the first meal is when it is over. Every mouthful a delight to be savoured. Everything is a treat to be relished. Mindfulness is savouring life.

# It's Unreal

## Realities of Life

> *Reality is that which, when you stop believing in it, doesn't*
> *go away.*
> – Philip K. Dick

When you think about reality where does your mind take you? Do you immediately go to your present circumstances and to what life has or has not given you? Or do you see reality as an amalgamation of true facts? An unequivocal, fixed framework which forms the visible, tangible and trustworthy 'real world' – where a tree is a tree and fish don't climb them. A public stage where reality states that sometimes the traffic lights fall in your favour and sometimes they don't. Not because you are blessed or marked, just because that is what they do. It is the real world which is made up of undeniable truths that apply to all of us, because when you get down to brass tacks, reality just 'is'.

And yet it also isn't. Because if there are 7.7 billion people now living on this planet, you can be assured that there are then at least 7.7 billion different realities. Each person has their own unique interpretation of what the reality of life actually is. Because we all see the world from our personal standpoint, and we each have our own story about the world that we have built up over the years, which we then put a label on and mark 'reality'. We can all find like-minded souls who will happily nod in agreement at our definition – they tend to be the people we like most, and end up being our friends. But although our take on life may be similar, there will always be aspects to each of our ideas of what reality is which remain unique.

The objective, straight-talking, 'call it as you see it' real world is not much more than a base layer to what most of us refer to as reality. It represents the fundamental reality which creates a framework for the public playing field we all live our lives on. Regardless of who we are in life and our position in it, regardless of what anyone says, it is not possible to ever have complete control of the playing field. None of us had a say in the family or environment we were born into or anything in our childhood. It is not solely down to us if we will win that promotion at work or if the person we love with all our heart will love us back. And the truth is that, even if we follow society's definition of success to the letter – ace our exams, get into the right crowd, acquire belongings others will envy or find global fame – there are absolutely no guarantees it will bring us lasting happiness or whatever it is that we want from our lives.

But part of the Great Wake Up is realising that most of our idea of reality is just that – an idea. It is a belief, a construction, a fiction on a par with the classics. We project our beliefs and opinions on to the 'real world' where pigs don't fly and we make it personal. What most people consider as reality says little about the 'real world' but everything about them. If we were aware of this there wouldn't be a problem, but we never question our own idea of reality. Which means we remain confined by our own limiting ideas: that reality is fixed a certain way, to one viewpoint, and that we have no choice but to go along with it. We don't realise that this one fixed viewpoint is actually our personal viewpoint and so by changing that viewpoint or choosing to have more than one, we can not only change but control much of our reality.

Our reality is made up of two parts and, as we have seen in earlier steps, we all live in two worlds: the public one we share and the private one that we don't. That said, we tend to treat them as one and the same. This is absolutely fine; in fact, it is as it should be – the world does not need to hear all our innermost thoughts. However, when our inner beliefs jar with how the outside world is, this can create real mental anguish. It can make us believe that either the world is against us or that there is something fundamentally wrong with us. Neither is true. However, when our two worlds are not aligned, the problem does not lie in the public world but our private one. The first thing we need to realise is that how we see the world is more important than anything that is actually going on in it.

Most of us assume that the outside world is the one we need to focus all our attention on if we want to have a wonderful life, and that it alone has the means within it to make us feel better. We assume that the outside world dictates whether our life is good or bad and whether we spend it being happy or not. In fact, the reason why our two worlds jar has little to do with the outside world and everything to do with our private inner world. Our inner world is the big boss. How we see reality is completely dependent on our state of mind at any particular time. For example, when you are in love, have just aced an exam or closed a deal, the world is a pretty wonderful place; the birds singing in the trees are a delight. When you have just had your heart broken, failed the exam or lost the deal, the world becomes a very different place and your feelings towards the birds singing in the trees may be a little different.

When we look to the world around us to improve our well-being or how happy we feel, we are focusing all our efforts on the wrong world. We are hooking all of our hopes on the world we cannot control at the expense of the one we can. It doesn't matter what wonders and delights we are offered, our state of mind – and only our state of mind – will decide whether we enjoy them. The only reality is that the outside world is powerless to truly change our life without the permission of our inner world. Thanks to the media we have endless examples which make its unyielding power undeniably clear – those with not much more than the shirt on their back who seem completely content, regardless of their lot in life, and those who are seemingly privileged with everything they could possibly want, who struggle with mental anguish and, try as they might, cannot find peace or happiness.

## Reviewing Your World

> *There are no facts, only interpretations.*
> – Friedrich Nietzsche

A lot of our mental anguish comes because we only know how to look at life in one particular way. For some that might be through an emotional filter; for others it may be a more pragmatic approach. This means that when our own viewpoint is the cause of our suffering, we have no choice but to endure it. Imagine walking down a path which starts to get really muddy. The kind of mud where each step you take is an effort and you think you are going to lose your boot. If you know of another path, you have a means of escaping the muddy nightmare – all you have to do is swap paths. But if the path is the only one you know, then you have no choice other than to slowly make your way through the thick mud and pray that at some point soon it comes to an end.

It is much the same when we are bogged down in a drama or an emotion. Everything slows down, our reality narrows and we become consumed by our feelings and oblivious to everything else. All we can see is the mud. When we are struggling in life, one of the quickest ways to escape the stranglehold is to change our standpoint and try to perceive the situation another way – pretty much any way other than the one being used. There are a number of ways you can do this, such as asking yourself a set of questions; approaching your situation with a sense of curiosity and objectivity in the same way you might inspect an object; or acknowledging your emotion and then asking yourself why the drama has affected you and why you feel so adamant. Is it a fear behind the emotion? Does it make you feel out of control? This is not about justifying your point of view, but rather trying to see more than your point of view. Being interested as to why you have this point of view and whether it is helping or hindering you. What does the drama look like from different viewpoints? If you are in an argument, can you see their point of view? As the Native American saying goes, 'Never judge another man until you have walked a mile in his moccasins.' How would a third party view it? We need to continue to challenge our own often habitual perspective. Do you need to be like an artist and step back from the canvas so you can see beyond the drama? Only by taking a step back can you pinpoint what exactly is causing you pain.

Everything in spirituality is about getting to the bottom of how and why we suffer. Not just understanding the root causes, but giving practical steps to really help us. One of the answers lies in a quote from Korean Zen master Seungsahn:

> 'Whether the world is empty or not, whether it exists or not, doesn't matter. What we call 'world' is only an opinion. Take away your opinion, then what? What is left? That is the point. Take away your opinion – your condition, situation – then your mind is clear like space. Clear like space means clear like a mirror. A mirror reflects everything: the sky is blue, tree is green, sugar is sweet. Just be one with the truth – that's Zen style. Only talking, talking no good. No truth.'

When we are struggling, one thing we can do is go back to the baseline of reality – that is, objective reality without your opinion of it. A tree is a tree, a fish is a fish and mud is mud. They are neither good nor bad, they just are what they are. Absolutely everything else which sits on top of this baseline is a personal interpretation; it is just your opinion. When you accidently step in a cow pat in your brand-new trainers on a country walk, it doesn't mean the world is out to get you. The pat wasn't strategically placed, the cows aren't all sniggering behind a tree. It's yucky and annoying, yes, but it's pointless to elongate your suffering any further by letting it ruin the rest of the walk or the day dwelling on it. As soon as we can recognise this, the power is back in our hands and we are free to say what stays and what goes. We can stop a lot of our own suffering by changing our interpretation. It doesn't mean our life will suddenly become devoid of drama or feeling, but it does mean that we know how to see through them, so they do not completely consume us.

As soon as you realise that reality is not a fait accompli, the illusion that reality is something that happens to you, and that you have little say in it, evaporates. It becomes plain that our experience of reality is down to us and that it is pretty pointless trying to change our life if we don't first change how we look at it.

Reality is like a kaleidoscope; the pieces of coloured fragments always stay the same, but what you see when they move, morph and merge depends on the position of the mirror reflecting them. In exactly the same way, how we see the world out there is a reflection of our internal world. In both cases, we are the catalyst – nothing can happen without our involvement. Just as we turn the tube which makes the pieces move, so the pieces that makes up our reality – people, events – will not change until we shift our perception of them.

## The Shamans' Way of Seeing

*Reality is only a Rorschach ink-blot.*
– Alan Watts

How we see life depends on the lens through which we look at it. Different lenses filter how we experience the world in different ways, and so it is important to make sure you are using the right one or, even better, realise that there is more than one.

When we change our perception of the events in our life our reality shifts. In exactly the same way as a camera can zoom in or pan out depending on the shot we want to take, we can do the same when it comes to our life. Just as you wouldn't put on a pair of reading glasses to look at the sunset over the horizon, we also know that sitting all day on a cushion chanting 'Om' is not going to pay the rent.

As obvious as it may seem, we often use the wrong filter: swiping to find our soulmate, trying to rationalise and make sense of depression or doing a full moon fire ceremony in a bid to manifest a mansion. We might see some change in the right direction, but this is because we have focused our intent; it is a hit-or-miss approach and there is an easier and far more reliable way to make use of the various lenses. Understanding the different levels of perception is invaluable. It is without doubt one of the most practical and powerful practices I know and one which has helped me through several tough times in my life.

I was introduced to the four levels of perception by my mentor, Alberto Villoldo, a Shaman elder and founder of The Four Winds Society. When I first heard Alberto describing the different ways of seeing reality, it was an 'aha' moment for me. It brought to life what, up until then, had been nothing more than an abstract concept which I had struggled to get my head around. For the first time, I had a way of mapping my own invisible inner world and really seeing how it manipulated my views of the world. The power in the way the Shamans map out our inner landscape is in its simplicity. They use colourful imagery which is easy to remember and quick to read. It is full of metaphors using nature and the animal kingdom to make complex concepts crystal clear, fast. The simplicity makes it accessible for everyone, regardless of age.

Alberto divides how we perceive reality into four levels:

1. The physical level, represented by the Serpent.
2. The psychological level, represented by the Jaguar.
3. The soul level, represented by the Hummingbird.
4. The spirit/energy level, represented by the Condor.

The animal archetypes used in the four levels of perception may seem somewhat exotic if you don't live in the rainforest or in a remote village high up in the Andes, but the sense they evoke is universal. We can all, with the help of a little imagination, conjure up a sense of what it might feel like to be the Serpent, belly to belly with the earth, only able to see what is directly in front of us, relying entirely on our instincts; or to be the Condor gracefully gliding high in the sky, circling and surveying the great expanse. Even if you struggle with visualising, you know logically that a serpent's experience of the world is not going to be anything like that of a condor's. Alberto's choice of archetypes is not random. They are there to stop the different levels simply being yet another intellectual concept and help us have a deeper sense of what each level actually feels like. The levels are like four filters which influence how we perceive our realities. The level of Serpent is the camera lens zoomed in so you can pick up the micro material details and the level of Condor is the lens zoomed out to give you a panoramic view of your life.

Once you understand the different levels we all use to perceive reality, it becomes obvious how our reality changes depending on how we choose to frame it. The following is my interpretation of the four levels of perception:

## The physical (Serpent)

At this level, reality is stripped back to the essentials and the world is made up of material. Our concerns at the physical level are focused on doing what needs to be done, devoid of any emotion or intellectual analyses. We are solely concerned with facts and function, putting one foot in front of the other and doing what has to be done. When we use this lens to filter reality, the world is whatever our senses tell us it is. It physically exists, there is no thought required. A tree is a tree. You can see it and you can touch it. This is the real world where when we cross the road we know to look left or right regardless of whether we are an enlightened being or not. At this level, we are a unique physical being in a world packed with other unique physical beings. When we look at the world through this lens, like the Serpent we are only concerned with our immediate needs, we don't save or hold visions for the future. Like the Serpent at this level, our senses and instincts are for the sole matter of survival. This is a perfect lens to use in a time of crisis, when fear and emotions are not just of no help, but are a handicap. As an explorer friend of mine once told me, the first rule of survival is to decide to survive. If you find yourself stuck on top of a mountain with the night drawing in, the last thing you want to be doing is panicking about whether you are going to make it through the night or not, wasting your energy stoking up a drama instead of finding wood for a campfire. You need a cold, ruthless focus on what needs to be done to survive through the night.

## The psychological (Jaguar)

At this level, we can still access the level of the Serpent but now we also have a full range of thoughts, feelings and emotions. There is more to the world than merely what our eyes can see. At this level, the language is words, intellectual thoughts, vision, ideas and emotions. Now science is a passion. As the American physicist, Richard Feynman, said, 'Physics is like sex: sure, it may give some practical results, but that's not why we do it.' When we use this lens, reality is subjective; everything becomes a personal interpretation as we see the world according to our beliefs and experiences. This is the level most of us know best. Now we can still see the tree as just a tree, but we can also project our thoughts and opinions on to it and decide whether we like it or not. We can critique it, style it and compare how we think it shapes up to other trees. At this level, the tree is not just a place under which we can shelter, it can be made into a stylish home. The fire is not just there to keep us warm, it is a place to sit by and share stories with friends and burn sausages.

The Shamans call this the realm of the Jaguar because here we look at reality with the curiosity of a cat. We are interested in exploring everything that there is to be seen. We don't simply react to our environment, we access our situation. Like the cat, we can be playful or retreat up a tree to lounge and watch the world go by.

## The soul (Hummingbird)

The level of the soul is a realm which lies beyond words. It is a place within us which is impossible to explain, unless you are a poet. It cannot be made sense of at the intellectual level and it cannot be analysed. We can access it through the song on the radio which seems to speak directly to your soul or the painting which stops you in your tracks. It is a profound realm where the only language is art, music, myth and ritual. When the soul is touched, it is a moment which evokes something magnificent that transcends the daily stuff and reminds you that there is so much more to life than the literal. It is a moment when time seems to stop still. At this level, we know we are part of something much bigger and more magnificent than our individual lives. We can experience it in any ceremony that moves us, a rite of passage or simply stopping to gaze up at the stars in the night sky. When we look at our reality through this lens, we start to perceive life as sacred. At this level of perception, we can enjoy the realms of Serpent and Jaguar, but we rise to where we can see the whole timeline of our life, the whole picture. The archetype for this level of perception is the Hummingbird. Observe how a colourful hummingbird moves and it is hard not to delight in nature's magic. One minute it is flying backwards, the next it is hovering in front of a flower. The hummingbird is one of the smallest birds and yet it achieves the seemingly impossible, migrating vast distances twice a year. At this level, life becomes an adventure and we are the hero in our own epic tale. At this level, the tree becomes more than just a tree, it is the Tree of Life; from acorn to oak, a timeless myth which speaks of a heroic journey, one we all must take.

## The spirit/energy (Condor)

The level of Condor encapsulates all the other levels of perception because, just as the Condor flying high in the sky can see beyond the horizon as well as its prey on the ground, we can zoom right in on the detail and we can pan right out to see the bigger picture. At this level, you are free from all your – and, for that matter, everyone else's – stuff. You know that your identity is part of the illusion, because at this level there is no 'I' – everything is connected. You have transcended dualism and time and gone beyond form. You are at one with the world. It is called by a number of names: spirit, pure awareness, no mind, Shoonya. Here you do not see the tree form; it is simply energy, a formless manifestation of consciousness. Imagine seeing the tree through an electron microscope. Looking through the microscope you can't tell that you are looking at a tree because you are too close to see its actual form. All you can see are atoms, molecules and energy – exactly the same components that make up everything, including us. At this level of perception, everything is the same. We are as much the mountain, the river, the tree, the flower as we are ourselves. We are the Condor with its majestic wingspan circling in the sky and the agile Jaguar gracefully making its way through the rainforest. When you perceive reality from this level, you are not just a part of nature and the flow of life; you *are* nature, you *are* the flow of life. You and the universe are one and the same.

## Playing with Perception

*Sometimes the situation is only a problem because it is looked at in a certain way. Looked at in another way, the right course of action may be so obvious that the problem no longer exists.*

– Edward de Bono

When the Shamans want to change their world, they change their perception of it. Knowing how to balance and shift perceptions is an important tool.

We are all familiar with the first two levels of perception – the physical and the psychological – and they tend to get our full attention. In today's busy world, however, the soul and spirit pretty much get ignored and we don't really put any value on them. We rarely give ourselves time to pause and daydream big, and, when we do, we squash our dreams and tell ourselves they are not real-istic. We rarely, if ever, look at our life as a whole or ask ourselves what kind of life we actually want; what would make us sigh with satisfaction when we are old and lying on our deathbed. As for spirit, well that's either just considered 'woo-woo mumbo jumbo' or something to keep separate from our everyday life. We all probably lean towards one level more than the others and live our life predominantly from there. Whether you are straight down the line by nature, or you hop from one drama to the next, or you see life as an adventure, or you are more interested in the inner world, we cannot rest in just what we know.

It is important to make sure no one level is ever hogging the microphone like that person on a bad karaoke night. For a fulfilling life they need to be equally balanced with each other. This is not some ladder system with the goal of finding your very own lofty cloud to lounge back on and be at one with the universe. No level is better than another; they are equally important and equally needed. Each level has its own insights. If there is a goal at all, it is to be at ease with each level of perception. Our rational, emotional, soul and spiritual selves all need to have their voice heard. Our rational self is invaluable, but we are more than walking computers. Not everything in our lives can be analysed or logically understood. A person may, on paper, have a perfect life and yet find themselves incapacitated with bouts of deep depression. If we try to rationalise everything in life, we starve the soul. When you can have the experience of each plane it is not about rejecting one plane in favour of another – you are simply able to make use of them and enjoy them all.

Unless you plan to emigrate to the Himalayas and take up home in a cave to meditate 24/7, you do not want to be permanently at the level of spirit. We have to live life in everyday reality, which involves having to deal with ordinary requirements, like the school run. However, nor do you only want to experience life at the physical level of Serpent, only concerned with a to-do list, devoid of emotions, visions and dreams.

Learning how to move from one level of perception to another is an empowering skill. Finding the right level of perception is equivalent to looking at a problem with fresh eyes. It will help and possibly remove the problem altogether by helping you see what to do. Whenever you feel as though you are struggling, for whatever reason, take a moment and look at the situation from each level. First notice the level of perception which is in control and then shift through the levels in much the same way you might go through the gears while driving. Often the simple act of looking at the situation from each level will be all you need to do to get unstuck. Imagine being stuck in traffic on the way to an important meeting. Your mind goes into a spin with a mixture of 'this can't be happening', 'my life is ruined' thoughts screaming in your head, as you sit beeping your horn in stationary traffic, stuck. This is not the time to be filtering reality through an emotional lens; if you do you will simply stoke the drama. Instead, remove yourself from the painful drama and use a more practical lens – make the call saying you are stuck in traffic and what time you think you will arrive. You can even go up into Condor and see the situation in proportion with the great scheme of life. All you need to do is take the drama and approach it from all four levels of perception. You will quickly be able to see where you are stuck and rebalance. It makes life a lot smoother for your friends and family as well. In my own life I have found that being able to perceive reality from different levels has actively helped me get through a crisis.

A few years back, I woke up in the middle of the night to a really loud gurgling sound coming from the pipes in my bathroom. Outside, the rain was coming down thick and fast. Before I was even fully awake or my brain could put two and two together, I was at the downstairs door, bucket in hand. There was probably no more than a sixty-second gap from my being fast asleep to bailing out the water that had started to come in from under the door. It was a reflex survival action – I was at the level of Serpent, following my instincts and doing what needed to be done, totally focused and devoid of any emotion. In that moment, my sole purpose was to deal with the situation at hand. As I realised later, my instincts were a little off as I was merely bailing the water back into the drain which was overflowing into my home, but that's another matter and I felt I was doing something significant at the time. It kept me busy in a time of crisis. When the water started coming in from every possible opening, it became obvious that bailing was futile, and my focus turned on getting everything I could off the floor and salvaging what I could. It was only when there was nothing more that I could do that I retreated to high ground, in this case upstairs, and could start to take in what was happening below. The moment I stopped, I came out of survival mode and the practical mind gave way to thoughts and emotions about the damage and the nightmare of sorting it out.

Knowing the four levels meant I could work with them and make the event as easy as possible for myself. I knew that I was better off for the time being remaining at the level of Serpent and that my emotions were only going to depress me. So, I reverted back to the literal level and continued to focus solely on the practicalities and just doing what needed to be done, one job at a time. Every now and then I would momentarily let myself stop and think about the implications of the flood. When the emotions felt less raw and blinding, I started to look at the situation properly from the level of Jaguar. The emotional drama around the flood settled. For the next couple of weeks, I filtered reality at these two levels. I wasn't ready to look at the bigger picture. I had no interest in seeing a deeper meaning in it or as part of my soul's 'journey'. But over time I did. I realised it had forced me to do a spring clean of my belongings. Also, as my practice room had been hit by the flood, I had had to create a makeshift one in my sitting room. The flood had forced me out of my fixed attitudes of what I needed to be able to do my work. It reminded me to be flexible, not to get fixed in my ideas. To be lighter on my feet in life. I started to look at the bigger picture. So, the dance became between the literal, emotional and soul levels. There were still things that needed to be done, but my emotions started to work with me rather than against me, and time off the hamster wheel gave me the opportunity to re-evaluate my priorities.

Finally, at Condor, I could see the whole picture and I also knew it was just life. The loss and damage weren't important, they were just things. From this perspective, the whole event ceased to be a drama and I could see the flood for the small event it actually was. Does that mean I am glad it happened? No. But knowing how to use the different levels of perception and move between them meant I didn't get stuck in the drama of the event ad infinitum, and so I didn't unnecessarily prolong my suffering.

This is a powerful resilience tool we can all use. Try it next time a drama, big or small, hits your world. Look at the situation through each of the lenses and you will see for yourself just how easy and effective this skill can be at saving you from becoming consumed by it and not being swept away by the tide of a drama for too long.

# Softening Your Grip

## Peeking around Corners

*One is never afraid of the unknown; one is afraid of the known coming to an end.*
– Jiddu Krishnamurti

The final part of the Great Wake Up is realising that, try as we might, we will never control life to a T. It is an illusion. But unlike the previous two steps, there is nothing deceptive about the illusion of control – it is purely a figment of the imagination, an illusion on a level with the emperor and his new clothes. We can invest to our heart's content in endless apps to help us keep a handle on things and learn yet more intricate methods to organise, box and label life. But if we overdepend on any of them, we are trusting life to be predictable – and it isn't. The nature of life is that it is in a constant state of change. Life cannot be reduced to a neat formula or confined to a carefully written out to-do list. As Woody Allen once said, 'If you want to make God laugh, tell him about your plans.'

It is part of the human condition, however, that we all want to feel that we are in control, otherwise we don't feel on solid ground and safe. There is an innate primal fear of the unknown, which was perhaps more immediately important for our ancestors, but still heavily influences how we choose to live our lives today. On some level, it makes sense that the better we know our environment, the better chance there is of making it through to tomorrow, and it is comforting not having to second-guess our every move. We want to get things right, because when we get things right, then our world is safe. So, as we make our way from child to grown-up, we develop our own ways of doing things and a feeling about the ways we like things to be. We create personal routines that give us a sense of security and mean we know where we are, how to be and what to do in any given moment. Until, that is, life throws us a curveball and we don't. Our safety structures fall apart, and we find ourselves floundering and grasping on to whatever we can to recover our sense of safety. It can be anything from a cancelled flight, when we need to reorganise our plans, to a sudden loss.

It is often the small stuff that trips us up. Details which really are totally inconsequential suddenly get blown out of proportion and become incredibly important and urgent because it is all we are capable of focusing on. We approach life with an ever-shortening fuse and a tolerance level scraping the floor. Nothing is good enough as we project our discomfort with the world on to everyone else. Or we choose to focus on anything which doesn't require any kind of emotional engagement from us, methodically going about our day with the same lack of life as an AI robot. In this scenario, we have closed down. When we need everything to be exact and 'just so', it is because we have got ourselves into a state where we feel we cannot cope if it isn't. So, when our inner Mary Poppins or tinpot dictator comes to the rescue and we find ourselves barking at everyone or puffing cushions for the umpteenth time, we can take it as a sign that we are floundering and scrambling any way we can to find our footing.

Feeling in a state of flux is by its very nature unsettling, so being busy can come as a relief as at least in the moment it makes us feel like we are doing something constructive. But all it really means is that we focus on everything but the real problem. Like the hamster keeping itself busy in the important job of running around its wheel, we can avoid looking at any underlying issues. We are distracting ourselves from ourselves. However bizarre it may seem to acknowledge, being consumed with worry can give us a false sense of control over our situation, because at least we get to be in control of the worrying. It also means that, while we are worrying, we don't actually have to take any action, which has some comfort when you just don't know what to do. But the comfort is short term. There is a quote by Corrie ten Boom, who helped many Jews escape the Nazis, which describes the debilitating effects of anxiety beautifully: 'Worry does not empty tomorrow of its sorrow, it empties today of its strength.' What we end up doing is shutting down our own instincts and intuition which, rather than helping, makes us feel more disconnected and, in turn, anxious because we lose our ability to sense anything at all. In the stress and anxiety, we lose touch with ourselves, which then makes us feel even less safe and so we feel the need to control even more tightly. It becomes a vicious circle.

It feels the same as when we don't move to our own drumbeat.

We feel like we are walking through life on eggshells, constantly trying to pre-empt what might be coming around the corner and, in doing so, we become even more anxious. It feels like nothing can help us to break free, settle our nerves or dissolve the anxiety while our mind is in a state.

First we have to stop – press the pause button on everything and step back. Then we need to decompress, release all the pent-up energy and reconnect with ourselves. The most immediate and effective way is to come back into the present moment. Come away from any thought and come back into the body. The quickest way is through our breath. If you are someone who by nature gets anxious, doing a short breathing meditation (like the one below) will not only help with the symptoms that come with anxiety, like shallow breathing and not being in the body, but over time will build up your resilience, so that when life does unsettle you, you can quickly find your equilibrium again.

Again, this is about setting new habits, so it makes an enormous difference showing up every day. It gives you a chance to ground yourself. It gives your mind a chance to take a few minutes to stand down and take a rest. When you do this, you are befriending your mind and you will feel the rewards over time. Remember, just as with a wild horse, it is a matter of building trust. The better you get to know your own mindscape, the more you will be able to relax.

## Square breath meditation

The following breathing meditation is highly effective when you are struggling with anxiety, because it gives enough for the mind to focus on, freeing you from whatever it is that is occupying your mind. It is a quick exercise and you really can do it anywhere, at anytime. This is important to know because when we are anxious, we tend to feel that we don't have time to do anything other than focus on how anxious we are feeling. It takes our full attention and we feel too jittery to believe we can be anything else, let alone settle. We are consumed by our anxious state.

This meditation takes under a minute to do. Its power lies in the fact that there is enough to catch the mind's attention and free you from being endlessly spun around in a toxic thought loop, but it is short enough to stop the mind wandering off. You can do this with your eyes open or shut.

- Consciously take a few slow, deep breaths.
- Then breathe in for the count of four, hold your breath for the count of four, exhale for the count of four, hold your breath for the count of four. This makes one full cycle.
- Repeat this four times.

You will feel calmer by the end, and the intensity of the anxiety will have lowered and possibly disappeared. You will certainly find it tough to go back to the exact train of thought or jitteriness you were feeling before. I do this same breathing exercise before every client session, but to the count of seven: inhale for seven, hold for seven, exhale for seven and hold for seven, seven times. It is a powerful mind cleanse.

## Grabbing at Air

> *He who binds to himself a joy*
> *Does the winged life destroy*
> *He who kisses the joy as it flies*
> *Lives in eternity's sunrise*
> – 'Eternity', William Blake

The Shamans of the Andes have a sweet yet profound practice of giving whatever they have become overattached to back to nature. They understand that the things in life that make us suffer can be as much our dreams as our nightmares. There are the physical or emotional pains and losses, but also the desires that we cling to or belongings we crave, that keep us separated from being in and enjoying the present moment. They do this by blowing their prayers into a 'kintu', a Quechua word for a sacred offering, which is made up of three carefully chosen coca leaves placed together. The three leaves represent the lower world where we hold our wounds from the past, the middle world where we live our lives today and the upper world, home to our destiny. In the act of blowing whatever it is that keeps us from not living fully now into the kintu, we break free from the hold the desire or hurt has over us, relinquishing any sense of our control to the universe and letting go of any yearned-for outcomes. Holding the kintu up in their hands, the Shamans first call in the sacred mountains (Apus), the sun (Inti), the moon (Killa), the stars (Chaskas) and Mother Earth (Pachamama) to be present. They then blow a desire, a hope, a dream, a pain, a toxic thought, or anything that is keeping them out of sync with the natural flow of life, into the kintu. Then they either chew the kintu, throw it in the air for the wind to take, or place it somewhere on the ground.

Most of us don't have a problem with change when it is of our doing, because we feel we are in charge of the outcome. The change has been our choice and so it feels within our control. When change isn't of our doing, however, and we have no control over it, it becomes daunting. It is hard to just go with the flow and take life as it comes. We all have things in our life that we like and don't want to change. This is fine and healthy. However, when our attachment to a person, dream, desire, fear, idea or belonging becomes so strong that it overshadows our world and keeps us fixated, it can cause us real suffering. When we become too attached, we are in danger of squeezing the life out of it. This does not mean that we have to avoid becoming attached to anything, it is simply a matter of being aware of how we hold our attachments – they are at the root of our suffering and, when we cling to them too tightly, they can stop us from really living freely. Everything has the potential to cause us suffering if we become too attached. It is like being bound to a sticky cobweb which holds you like glue and you live out of the natural flow of life.

One way to see suffering is as the psychological version of physical pain. So, if you don't like going to the dentist, the moment you see in the diary that you have a routine check-up, the suffering starts. You start worrying and, if you are like me, the feeling of dread takes over. The worry and dread are just thoughts, but these thoughts hang over you right up until you actually walk into the dentist practice. Pain, on the other hand, is the moment the dentist starts removing a nerve in your tooth before the local anaesthetic has taken effect. Unlike pain, which normally has a precise beginning and ending, suffering is much harder to break free from, because it is like a constant hum with no clear edges or ending.

The Buddha realised all this sitting under his bodhi tree. At the heart of the Buddhist teachings are the Four Noble Truths, which look at all the different ways we can suffer and, more importantly, how to overcome them. The Buddha recognised that all emotions have the potential to cause us deep suffering, even love. He saw that suffering extends way beyond physical pain or disease and that it is an emotional anguish which will survive as long as we feed it with the energy of our thoughts. Quite simply, when we refuse to accept the laws of nature, we open ourselves to suffering.

Suffering has many guises. Loss and heartbreak are easy ones to identify, but it takes subtle forms too. Suffering lives in the dreams we cling to, the belongings we desire or maybe the recognition we are craving. Our suffering is in how we bind ourselves to a tragic event. It is the reaction to a feeling of loss which seems to stop life in its tracks, freezing us in time. When we are in this place, we don't know how we will break free, or even if we want to break free. It can come from clinging to that perfect moment against which you then compare all future great moments and find them wanting. It can come from yearning for love or, once you have found love, the fear that it will slip through your fingers somehow. It can come from loving someone so much that you live with the constant fear that something might happen to them. It is believing you cannot be happy until you reach a certain status, get that job, own that Ferrari or lose ten kilos, or once you have got these things, the worry that you might lose them.

Suffering can come from the pain when you realise that the momentary thrill of having the status, the Ferrari or losing ten kilos hasn't filled the emptiness you thought it would or soothed that deep inner ache. If we grip too tightly to a person, an event, a moment, a possession, we are in effect refusing to accept that a mood will change, a relationship will evolve and objects can break.

When we blow the things that make us suffer into a kintu, we symbolically sever our attachment to the dream or the nightmare. It is like telling the universe what you want or don't want, but then letting go of the outcome. By breathing it into the leaves you are also breathing movement back into the places in your life where you have become stuck. It is an act of freeing yourself so that you can reconnect with the present moment.

## Andean Shaman kintu ritual

This is a ritual, so take your time over each stage. The traditional kintu is made from coca leaves which are not available in the UK, so I like to go and pick small leaves from the ground in the park near where I live. Take time to pick leaves in the best possible condition. You don't need them to be 'perfect', just ones which aren't split or partially broken. If they are different sizes, put the largest one at the back and the smallest one at the front. I recommend going out on your own to find the leaves as it is a nice meditation of its own; a chance to let the attachment surface.

Aim to simply make one kintu for the first big attachment which comes to mind. Sit somewhere quietly and really engage in how this attachment is affecting the natural flow of your life. Notice how much energy, attention and time you give it.

- Holding the kintu, call in places in nature that matter to you. The Andean Shamans call in the sacred mountains (Apus) which they live next to and hold power for them, but you can call in anywhere which is special to you. Either recognised places of power like Stonehenge in England, Uluru in Australia or the Ganges in India, or the land around where you grew up. It's your choice. Pick places which hold a power in you and have an energy with which you resonate.

- Then take the kintu in your hands by the stem with the leaves pointing up, close your eyes, connect with whatever it is that is causing you to yearn, anguish or feel pain, and blow it into the leaves.

- When you have given the energy of your suffering to the kintu, give it back to nature. As the chances are you not using coca leaves, do not chew the kintu. Give it to the wind or place it somewhere outside that feels right.

As with all Shamanic rituals, the structure is not rigid. Do not worry about making a mistake or getting it wrong. It is all about intention not perfection.

## Crossing the Line

> *There is but one freedom, to put oneself right with death.*
> *After that, everything is possible.*
> – Albert Camus

When it comes to our primal fear of the unknown, the greatest fear for most of us is death. We spend our life in a constant rush to get somewhere else, seeing the present moment as simply a means to an end, never quite taking on board exactly what the end goal actually is. Death is the proverbial elephant in the room which we try to squeeze away in a cupboard, in the hope that if it is out of sight it won't happen. It is not quite a taboo subject, but no one really wants to talk about death and, when someone does, they are either considered to be at best depressing or, at worst, macabre. We can bio hack away to our heart's content, grasping like a terrier to the ankles of life in a bid to defy time and remain forever young, but regardless of whether we have achieved enlightenment or are pumped with preservatives, our bodies will one day expire. Whether you see death as a lights out termination or a transition, like the caterpillar who doesn't realise it is about to become a beautiful butterfly, falls to your individual belief. However, much more important than our concerns as to what does or doesn't happen to us when our bodies stop, is not allowing a fear of death from keeping us from feeling fully free and alive while we are still living.

The Shamans believe that until we 'die to' everything we believe ourselves to be, our idea of who we think we are – our identity, our beliefs and our conditionings – we cannot truly live. It is a paradox, but dying to the idea of ourselves is the very thing that brings us alive. For many people, the first time they really start living life with gusto is when they have been forced to meet death face-to-face and have lived to tell the tale. The experience frees them from the stifling grip of fear, the 'shoulds' and 'shouldn'ts', and all the rules of engagement which we pick up and carry as we go through life. However, we don't have to wait for a life crisis to start living life with a real sense of freedom. We also don't have to continually think up death-defying feats like playing tag with great white sharks. We simply have to make sure we are not living life on automatic pilot so, when we do get to our last breath, we are not left wondering what it was we exactly did in our life.

When you look back at your life to date, there will already be plenty of things which once defined your world and that you thought were essential, but which have now fallen away and died. It is a relief to no longer be caught up with the same worries and concerns that consumed us when we were young. We can look back bemused by how unimportant everything we considered at the time to be of life and death importance actually was. We can also look back and see where our fears and/or insecurities have kept us from moving forward at different times in our life and kept our world small. It is never too late to unhook and free ourselves from outdated beliefs. When we do, our world opens up even more. Perhaps our last exhale is simply another hook to free oneself from.

While your idea of death may be as a finite moment, it is not the stranger you may think it is. It is a fallacy to think you have to wait for the Grim Reaper to pitch up to know death, because it already plays a part in your everyday life. In fact, it is an experience we have every single day. Every night we die to the day; we close our eyes and shut down our senses to the world. When we fall into a deep sleep we disappear from our life as we know it and travel to the unknown. Each night we do not know if we will get to visit the world of dreams that we could never find while awake or simply experience a relaxing blank.

Even when we feel like a bush fire has swept through our life and all we can immediately see is devastation, just like a real bush fire there will be new growth making its way through the burnt debris. Everything comes and goes as part of a continual cycle of transformation. Like push/pull, yin/yang or inhale/exhale, birth and death are part of life. It becomes clear when you see them as part of a cycle rather than a straight line. They exist together and they keep the cycle turning. They are part of an eternal continuation. In every breath there is a small birth and death – after your next exhale, don't inhale and this will become clear. One thing is for sure, with death comes birth. They are bound together like Siamese twins. You cannot have one without the other. As you read this, thousands of cells in your body are dying and thousands of cells are being born. We continue to evolve within the transitions. There are no finite moments. Just as we existed before we were born, it is fair to assume we will exist after we die, and that life is continually transforming. In the same way the cloud in the sky becomes the rain which becomes the puddle little children play in or the ice in your cocktail on a hot summer's evening, maybe we too have an ongoing adventure once we leave our bodies. I may have trained as a Shaman, but as I am not a dead Shaman, I don't know.

## Constant Change

*No man ever steps in the same river twice, for it's not the same river and he's not the same man.*
– Heraclitus

Wherever there is life there is movement, and like birth and death, one cannot happen without the other. The timetable will vary between your mobile phone, a moth or a mountain, but no matter how seemingly invisible the change is, everything in the world is in a constant state of flux. Nothing in life is permanent or fixed. We can intellectually understand that impermanence is a cycle of birth–death–birth, but most of us prefer to just focus on what we think is the better half of the cycle: on birth rather than death, and the ups rather than the downs. However, it is only when we can accept the whole cycle and stop resisting the less appealing parts, that life actually starts to ease up.

Try as we might to get life to move at a pace which suits us, everything has its own time and these individual timings cannot be forced or controlled. You cannot open a flower with a hammer, and even if you decided to go around sticking the leaves back on to the trees because you prefer spring to winter, still winter will come. When we let go of our stranglehold on life, we allow an effortless flow back into it.

Life is a dance, so we need to be flexible and light-footed and, as we adapt to its varying rhythms, we need to have a nimble mind to be able to adjust accordingly. When we become rigid or adamant that an event needs to be a particular way, we separate ourselves from the flow. It is like a dancer standing still because they can't hear the music; it cuts us off from our own natural flow of life and we can find ourselves continually struggling to find where to put our feet. It's helpful to look at it as the difference between concrete and water. Where water reacts with its environment, concrete stands separate. We want to be more like water, so we don't lose our ability to make use of our instincts and senses to help us when things don't go to plan.

Change is not only inevitable, it is the air which breathes life into life. There is an 'aha' moment when we realise that we don't need to control life, we just need the ability to adapt and go with it. When we feel groundless, we need to learn to fly.

Even when change is not of our choosing and it spins us out of control, we can lean into it. If you imagine change like water flowing in a river, we don't need to fight the current and try to swim against it. Nor do we have to try to control it by grabbing hold of every overhanging branch as we pass. If we do either we will simply exhaust ourselves and make our time in the river a nightmare. But if we let go and let the river carry us, it becomes effortless and, when we want to take a break, all we need do is swim to the side and rest a while on the riverbank. This is meditation – a chance to press pause on our everyday life, step out of the river and take a moment to be still.

Unexpected change keeps a spontaneity in life, which keeps us on our toes. It reminds us that our life is not a two-dimensional list of things to tick off (with all the suffering which happens when we take this approach); it is an epic adventure full of mysteries we don't fully understand, made up of endless twists and turns. What is more, it will continue to push us out of our comfort zone and encourage us to experience life beyond our own limited knowledge of it. Years back when I tried my hand at golf, someone told me to hold the club like I might hold a tiny little bird in the palms of my hands. Grip too tightly and I might kill it, too loosely and it might fly away. The tip stuck with me. It didn't help me with golf, but it has helped me in life.

## Travelling Light

> *Life has become immeasurably better since I have been forced to stop taking it seriously.*
> – Hunter S. Thompson

Keeping a control on life can become a very serious affair, too serious. It is very easy to get caught up in the importance of a drama or a deadline and lose touch with our lighter self. This is a serious matter because it is essential to our well-being to have fun. Whenever the signs start popping up that you might be getting a little overwhelmed by the demands of your day-to-day life and you feel the whole joy of life has evaporated, head straight to whatever it is that makes you laugh. Because the fastest way to 'let go', 'flow', 'just relax' or 'find yourself again' is through laughter. The effects are immediate. The body will unwind and balance will be restored.

We take life very seriously and get overanxious about getting everything right, but we can also take ourselves far too seriously. It is easy to be offended by anything and everything that affects our sense of who we think we are, but really the only person this actually hurts is ourselves. Being able to laugh at life and ourselves is incredibly freeing.

We all probably know people following a spiritual practice or just trying to do life well, who have fallen into a trap of maybe being a little too strict about what they can and can't do: wanting the cup of coffee or the cocktail, but worried that it is not good for them or thinking it shows them as not being truly spiritual; always worrying whether they are doing as much as they think they should be. The whole purpose of all spiritual teachings and practices is to enhance your life, not restrict it; to help you find freedom in your life, not to put you in yet another cage. Spiritual teachings are there to help keep us in balance and show us how to recover that balance when we fall. To bring a profound happiness into life. Sometimes spirit is best served in a glass with ice and lemon, surrounded by your friends.

Life will throw at you whatever it throws at you, and sometimes laughter is a more helpful reaction than earnestness. It is certainly one of the most effective ways to release mental tension. The benefit of keeping a light heart is the positive effect it has on our well-being and our spirit.

In truth, laughter is probably about as spiritual as you can get. One of the greatest meditations there is happens in the middle of a belly laugh. Because, when you really laugh, for those few moments you are actually in a deep meditative state. It is impossible to laugh and think at the same time. During a belly laugh is probably one of the few times we can all experience the mind going completely quiet.

The idea that to be spiritual means you need to approach life in an earnest, solemn, worthy, 'don't make me smile I am being very spiritual' way is possibly the funniest idea of all. You only have to look at photos of His Holiness the Dalai Lama, along with other great spiritual leaders, always smiling or laughing to see that this can't be true. The common theme between all the wisest folk I have had the good fortune to study and work with is that they all share a childlike quality and a lightness of spirit. They are in touch with the sweetness of life because they are able to flow with life. It doesn't mean they do not take their work seriously, they just don't take themselves seriously. This light-heartedness doesn't mean that they don't have their own concerns and struggles to deal with, they simply know that worry and angst will do nothing to help them. All it will do is deplete them of energy they would rather use elsewhere.

Following a spiritual practice or simply making use of the teachings and practices mustn't feel like a chore or yet another thing to put on your personal should-do list. When we are in balance, when we have found our natural flow, then spirituality and life are one and the same. Being spiritual is not a way of being. It *is* being. When we are in our flow, we are no different to the greatest spiritual leaders of the past because we are not in our own way. Keeping a light touch means staying humble. Life is to be enjoyed and a sense of playfulness, whatever your age, is a healing tonic to life's stresses. A big healing can be found in lightening up.

# Still You

## An Infinite Stillness

*We come spinning out of nothingness, scattering stars like dust.*

– Rumi

The next four steps are all about remembering and reconnecting. Rediscovering a stillness which we all have deep within us, that exists beyond the cascade of thoughts and actions and sensory attractions of the world around us. It is realising that we are not a separate entity plodding through life on our own, but part of an extraordinary web of creation, and that we are connected to something much larger and more magnificent than our small everyday worlds. It is remembering we are not just part of nature, we *are* nature; just as the waves are not separate to the sea, they *are* the sea.

In this stillness we reconnect to the natural consciousness which runs through all of us and gives us life. The constant pure flow of awareness which runs behind our idea of who we think we are – the masks we wear, the stories we tell, the things we believe or don't.

Stillness is your very own secret superpower. It is not simply a respite or a sanctuary from the demands of your life, it opens you up to an infinite source from where you can find inspiration, meaning and purpose. It is a limitless source deep within you from where your genius arises.

## The Sound of Silence

*An old silent pond . . .*
*A frog jumps into the pond,*
*splash! Silence again.*
– 'The Old Pond', Matsuo Bashō

Imagine diving into a beautiful blue sea from a boat on a hot summer's day. All around you the sea is full of life and activity. Big anchored boats sway, with people sunbathing on deck; colourful little fishing boats come and go in between. There are sailing boats, windsurfers, the sound of jet skis somewhere in the distance, little groups chatting as they swim around the bay and the sounds of children whooping with delight as they play in the little waves by the shore. Take in everything going and coming from each and every direction. Draw on all your senses to be there now – take in all the different sights and sounds, the smell of the sea and how your body feels in the cool, fresh water. Then, when you are ready, let yourself drop down. As you drop just under the surface, you become surrounded by loads of tiny fish, some pretty, some less so, all darting around at speed. Some grabbing food from the surface, others simply busy in the act of darting. Then let yourself sink a little lower. Now you notice there is more space between the fish, you see the odd bigger one moving a little slower, with more confidence and purpose. Now let yourself drop down further and, as you do, notice how a whole world opens up. You notice a quiet stillness. But this isn't a stillness akin to the heavy, thick relaxation you might feel when plonked in front of the telly after a big Sunday lunch or just before you fall asleep at night. This stillness is clear and fresh. It feels natural, like you have stepped into timelessness. Everything around you is very much alive and so are you. Everything is calm. As you settle on the seabed you can still see the world above, but you can also now see things which could only have been imagined if you had stayed above the surface.

Everything on the surface – all the different boats and all the people – is all the external noise in our lives vying for our attention. Grabbing our senses whichever way we turn. This is the everyday traffic, not only the literal noise of daily life but the news, opinion, comment, gossip, phone calls, emails and appointments. All of them are attention-grabbing, some fun, some not. The little fish darting around just below the surface are our thoughts and feelings which feed off all the different things that happen to us, constantly reacting to the world and the different bits and pieces of daily noise. They represent all the stuff at the front of our minds which we chew over or which chews us over.

The slower bigger fish which we pass are the limiting beliefs and conditionings which have shaped us. They have less to do. Their job is merely to remind the fish above of their presence and they do so by the shadows they throw. At the deepest level is a quiet, a stillness. It is a cleansing silence which perfectly balances the world above.

The surface world is so busy, we don't think beyond whatever is bobbing along on the top or isn't within plain sight. Everything at the surface level constantly demands our attention, and we can forget that if we just drop a little deeper and slow down, we can reconnect with this stillness whenever we want to. Just as we can't see the life along the seabed when we try to look down from the surface, we cannot experience the worlds which exist within 'being' when we are always busy 'doing'. If we want to, we have to pull ourselves away from all the attractions and do it. When we do, we invariably wonder why we don't do it more often because the stillness not only offers up new dimensions to explore, but is a nourishing respite.

The stillness is an infinite space; a realm where we can step out of time into an alert stillness. In the stillness is freedom. It is often referred to as 'no mind' – a state of consciousness where we transcend the 'I' and experience oneness with the world. We cannot exist without it any more than the waves can exist without the sea. It is part of us, and we are a part of it.

## The Dance

*He who lives in harmony with himself lives in harmony with the universe.*
– Marcus Aurelius

At the heart of all the ancient spiritual traditions are teachings and practices created to help us reconnect with this inner stillness. If you read spiritual books or follow a particular tradition, you will often hear this stillness being described as 'sacred', because it describes a flow of consciousness which is also often referred to as 'awareness' or 'true nature'. It is a universal spirit/life force which flows outside of our concept of time and runs through each and every one of us, feeding our imagination and connecting us to something much larger than ourselves.

Tapping into this universal energy is the holy grail for any spiritual seeker on a quest to find purpose and the meaning of life. And it is why some of us travel around the world trying to sate an inner niggle which tells us we are not complete. We can see that sense of wholeness and calm in the serene monks sitting in meditation and the wizened sages with their gentle, all-knowing expressions. They all seem to embody a profound timeless wisdom that we recognise, but maybe can't quite remember if this is something that we have too. It is. In fact, stillness is not something we actually have to go in search of because we all have it. Even when we are going through our worst times and feel at our most disconnected, it is always there. We couldn't lose it even if we wanted to, because it is the very thing that breathes life into us. So, the spiritual quest may seem about the silliest quest anyone could embark on – running around in search of something we already have – but this journey is by no means some time-wasting merry-go-around. It is essential. It is also full of experiences you will have nowhere else and it can be a lot of fun. Yes, it is true, you don't need to go to a remote mountain top to find it, nor do you need to have it transmitted by a guru, but just as you might employ a coach to help you in business or take a guide if you want to hike in a remote area, it's smart to get guidance from someone who has the knowledge. Even knowing that the journey is going to take you in a full circle and simply reveal something to you which was yours anyway. It is like rediscovering a forgotten natural water spring.

The benefit in knowing how to connect with our inner stillness is immeasurable. Like the mountain which stands silent and strong in all seasons, we can also remain still when we are surrounded by noise and chaos. Imagine not being spun out by the frenetic energy of a group of young children endlessly running around you on a sugar high. Our stillness gives us a stability which ensures that none of the small stuff life throws at us will be remotely troubling. Even when our head is being bombarded by an onslaught of thoughts, much like the mountain in the midst of a blizzard, the stillness remains. This is important to know because it would seem that the pace and demands of our lives today have a steadfast determination to keep us spinning as far away from this stillness as possible.

As the world continues to create more and more ways to distract us, our ability to concentrate on any one thing for more than a few seconds has pretty much evaporated. According to scientists, our attention span is now shorter than that of a goldfish. They can manage nine whole seconds before their mind wanders, whereas we allegedly only make it to eight. This is not a jibe at the modern world or a romantic notion that our ancestors had lives better than we do, they didn't. Advancements in living are extraordinary and exciting, but we need to remember that the surface world is only half the picture.

The Tàijítú is the yin-yang symbol taken from Daoism, an ancient Chinese philosophy which reflects the art of balance. It is made up of a circle divided by two swirls. Yang is the white swirl which represents doing, dynamism and fire. Yin is the black swirl and represents non-doing, the softness of water and stillness. Each swirl has a dot of the opposite within it to show that within each is the other. They are two opposing forces which are inter-dependent. They are as integral to each other as day and night and of equal importance like the sun and the moon. This has nothing to do with one being good and the other bad, or one being better than the other – they are equally essential. As a bodybuilder knows, the muscle is formed when the body is resting, not when you are actually pumping the weights in the gym. So, to bring yin into your life is not an advert to kick back and do nothing; just as yang needs the balance of yin, yin needs the structure of yang. A cup is empti-ness (yin) with a structure (yang) built around it – you need both to be able to drink your morning cup of tea.

The material world around us is the yang to the yin of our own inner stillness. When we are disconnected from this stillness, we feel incomplete; we sense that something in our life, however full it might be, is missing. It is a feeling of unquenchable emptiness and a sense of disconnection which we can never quite put our finger on, because most of us are all yang. We are out of balance.

It is pretty obvious that one cannot exist without the other, but our modern world prefers to ignore this. When we are yin, we are receptive; it is listening, whereas yang is talking. But we are only all 'doing', because we seem to think that just 'being' is another word for laziness. If we are all one and little of the other, it isn't all that surprising that we feel out of balance. Like the flame that burns too fast, we are burning ourselves out. It makes the fact that so many of the world's population now struggle with chronic fatigue, depression and anxiety a little more understandable. If we won't put yin into our lifestyle and calm down at least a little, which includes our overactive minds, the body will put some yin in for us and, if it has to, forcibly slow us down. The problem is that the emphasis around our whole education in the West is yang, so we are never taught about the value of balance and of how to recalibrate when we lose it.

'Being' compliments 'doing'. We know this. We just don't know how to do this in a way which doesn't seem heavy or dull or triggers our fear of missing out. Just as too much yang can knock us off balance, so can too much yin. Lack of any action or too much passivity in how we approach our life is not the answer to balance and fulfilment. We need both. When we find it it feels 'just right' – as Goldilocks discovered in the three bears' house.

When you think of balance, don't see it as the balance a tightrope artist needs; it is not that precarious – there is a rhythm to it, a natural ebb and flow. We are not trying to walk a never-ending straight line. There is no need to see life as a perpetual challenge. It is about being in harmony, in a natural flow. It is a dance and, like any good dancer, we may have to be light on our feet so we can ad lib a little when the music changes. When our lives are in balance, there is an ease to it. When there is balance, we can access the stillness.

## Slow and Simple

> **Be still. Stillness reveals the secrets of eternity.**
> – Lao Tzu

We can blast through life like a bullet train, but the faster we go the less we are able to experience anything other than the speed itself, and our life becomes increasingly streamlined and small. It is pretty difficult to hold on to anything when it is going at speed, so it is unsurprising that if you decide to race through your life, you can be fairly certain that you will lose touch with pretty much everything in it, including yourself. Anyone who has looked out of the window of a speeding train knows how the landscapes become an indefinable blur.

Do you ever ask yourself, why the rush?

If we are always focused on getting somewhere else, we never get to enjoy either the present moment or, for that matter, wherever it is we are looking to go, because as soon as we do get there, our minds will already be long gone, focused on the next and then the next, and so on.

The fuller and faster our lives are, the less chance we have of coming close to finding stillness. It remains nothing more than a nice idea – one which we don't have time for. Our mind's demand to be kept occupied keeps us apart from this inner stillness and, without a centre to stabilise us, we feel not just discombobulated but lost. The more disconnected we feel, the more susceptible we become to a smorgasbord of neurosis. It is a dis-ease which comes from being disconnected from our core and the inner stillness.

When you feel you have lost a sense of yourself or you find yourself wondering, 'What is it all for?' and you want to bring purpose and value back into your life, there are two things you can do which will have an immediate effect. The first one is to slow down and the second is to simplify your life. In the same way that you might minimise your wardrobe, minimise your life. Take out all the extra things which are taking up valuable space. It is true: less is more, much more. As soon as you start to notice that you are feeling more anxious than normal or your moods have gone south, take it as a cue to embrace the minimal. Pare right back and consciously slow down until you have regained your balance. Being able to slow down is a basic function of most things in life, but we don't think about it in terms of our own person. It is why cars have brakes and Usain Bolt doesn't sprint marathons. Life is not a race and you are not a camel.

Just as the muscles in your body need a chance to rest, so does your mind and, contrary to belief, the only time your mind truly gets an opportunity to rest is in meditation. Sleep rests the body, but it can be just as tiring a time for the mind as it processes your day as the day was itself. Again, this doesn't have to mean a 'sit on a cushion with a straight back in the lotus position repeating a mantra' meditation; it can be doing simple things like making your daily commute less of a dash and more a chance to look around and notice what is going on in the world around you. An easy exercise to do is slowing your walking down to the pace of your heartbeat. It may mean you get to the office a few minutes later, but your mind will be a lot sharper when you do arrive and your journey a lot more pleasurable. When your mind is really racing and you feel like the world is coming down on top of you, a few minutes focusing on your breath will help you recalibrate.

## Breath mountain meditation

This breathing exercise is a great one to do when you find everything has sped up too much and you feel you are heading towards a wormhole. Ideally you want to do it sitting down.

- Take a few deep breaths, inhaling through the nose and exhaling through the mouth. Make some exaggerated sighs as you exhale; they are genuinely effective. It is important to make a sound when you sigh – your body will take it as a cue to relax. Do at least three rounds of this before starting the actual exercise.
- When you are ready, let your breathing fall into its natural rhythm, inhaling and exhaling through your nose.
- Now take a deep in-breath to a slow count of two and exhale for a slow count of three; then breathe in for the count of three and exhale for the count of four; breathe in for the count of four and exhale for the count of five; breathe in for the count of five and exhale for the count of six.
- Continue increasing until you can no longer do it without fear of gasping. As you focus on your breathing let your mind have a rest.

When you are finished with the exercise, don't rush to move. Imagine reaching the top of a mountain – stay for a moment more to enjoy the stillness the breathing will have opened up. Enjoy the mental silence. If your mind wants to jump back into action, take a minute more and go through the five senses meditation on page 22. Notice the space that has formed in your mind before the thoughts cut in again.

## Creating a sanctuary

When our mind is clear and fresh and quiet, it is like a still lake which reflects its surroundings – the trees around it, the sky, the moon. It sees everything. But when the lake is disturbed, the only thing the lake can see is itself. When our mind is busy, we can't see beyond our own thoughts.

This is the reason why spiritual folk throughout the centuries have been retreating to caves, huts in nature, monasteries and convents for extended periods of time. It is probably one of the oldest spiritual practices there is. Some are so keen not to be distracted that they retreat to one-room huts and, once they have entered, they brick up the entrance. But none of them make a retreat to get to the top of some 'how worthy can you be' leader board or even to bag a prize spot in the afterlife. They do it because they want to experience other dimensions of life which are impossible to access when everything in life is tempting you with distraction. It may seem like you need to be some hardcore nutter to do a retreat like this. You probably do; it is not for the enthusiastic novice. However, we can have an idea of the altered states the solitude creates without going to this extreme. When people talk about having had a 'mystical experience', they have momentarily accessed the dimensions these hermits may be inhabiting.

Nowadays retreats have become mainstream. However, when we think of a retreat it is normally a week somewhere beautiful with a bit of yoga and someone cooking delicious, nutritious meals. They are a chance to get away from it all, where we can surrender our lives to a simple routine and spend the week wondering why we don't do it more often. We promise ourselves that, when we get home, we will keep up our new healthy habits and a year later we find ourselves making exactly the same promises. It is pretty easy to feel calm and at one with the world when we are sitting in our five-star cave overlooking a secluded beach with very little to irritate us except perhaps the odd mosquito. We have retreated from normal life. The trick is to be able to do this when life is upside down and being pulled inside out. We need to be able to access our inner stillness every day, amidst the chaos and noise.

A meditation practice is a retreat in itself. It is a moment when we retreat from the day and reconnect with ourselves. The more we consciously withdraw from the outside world to focus our attention inwards, the more likely we are to experience a stillness, regardless of what we are doing. Just as the workout in the gym continues once you have left, the stillness in our meditation also stays with us.

If you feel your life is lacking some of this nectar, start with simply creating a daily retreat and customise it to suit you. It doesn't have to be hardcore – make it doable for you. There are no brownie points on offer, so make it something you can relish rather than dread. Switch it about. I personally recommend a meditation of just sitting. As the late Dilgo Khyentse Rinpoche said, 'Meditation could be said to be the Art of Simplicity: simply sitting, simply breathing and simply being.' Make it your sacred time of just being quiet. It doesn't have to be a set meditation technique. Maybe do a digital detox for a few hours a day, go for a quiet walk without your phone or music, or have a long bath. A retreat at home is making a commitment to press pause and stop for a certain amount of time in the day. Do it for a week – it will have an impact. Don't expect to keep it going as a daily habit, though if you can then great. It also doesn't need to be solemn or earnest. I know someone who every morning at 11am lights up a big cigar. For the duration of that cigar, they simply sit and enjoy smoking it peacefully without any business interruptions. It is their daily ritual. When it is finished, they go back to their day.

## Mind the Gap

*Your sacred space is where you can find yourself again and again.*

– Joseph Campbell

Native American Shamans see the pause between the in-breath and out-breath as a sacred space. Focusing on this space is a meditation technique which allows us a moment of no-thing. In that moment we can vanish – there is no sense of a separate self, there is only an awareness. In the gap between the in- and out-breath, there is a full emptiness – as full as a pregnant pause. The Japanese have a similar concept called 'Ma' – negative space. The space creates a shape of its own as it forms between two structures, whether they are flower stems or two pieces of furniture. It is part of the aesthetic – an art form in itself. It doesn't just add depth and dimension, it is the emptiness full of possibilities. 'Minding the gap' is an appreciation that the space between things is as important as the things themselves. It is the silence between two notes which create music, the pause before a word to evoke something more than the word can say alone. The space between words or music notes is as important as the words or notes themselves. In between everything there is a gap. It is the yin. It is the stillness in a blank. It is easy to overlook because it is no thing, it does not seem of any importance, but the space is not a pointless void. We focus on what is and forget the grace which exists in what isn't: the words not said, the dramatic pause, the momentary reflection which opens you up to a whole other dimension.

## Sacred space meditation

In this next meditation the focus is on the gap between two thoughts. You can do this sitting or lying down, wherever you can be comfortable, but preferably not in a position which will have you snoring within a few moments!

- Let your eyes close. First focus on your body. Watch your breath – do not try to change it; simply watch your body breathing. Enjoy the sense of stillness of having to do absolutely nothing.

- Bring your awareness to your mind. Notice your thoughts – just watch them coming and going in the same way you would watch birds flying past, without any need or desire to engage with them. Have the sense that you are watching your thoughts from a distance so you can see each thought as a separate entity.

- Now focus on the space, however small, between one thought and the next in the same way you might focus on the space between one bird and the next as they pass. Mind the gap. Put your attention on to the space between the two. Let the thoughts become book ends to the space in between. Enjoy the stillness and silence in this space where there is no-thing.

- Let the gap become wider as if the space is pushing the thoughts further apart. Imagine what it would be like to dive into this pool of space. Notice how it feels to be in no-thing. As the next thought tries to grab your attention, look for the line which marks where it ends and the space starts.

This does not always need to be a formal meditation. Once you get used to it you can start looking for the end of one thought and the gap before the next one starts whenever you feel like it. Play with it.

## Superpower

*The moment you doubt whether you can fly, you cease for ever to be able to do it.*
– J. M. Barrie

As important as it is for our well-being to know stillness, it would be wrong to think of it simply as a respite or a sanctuary. When you access the stillness, it opens you up to an entirely new dimension. Possibly the best way to see this 'stillness' is as a state of awareness without thought, where the mind makes no attempt to obstruct you from a deep dimension of emptiness where creativity and moments of genius can arise. We all know it is in the quiet moments when we are not trying to find the answer that we find it. The light-bulb moments when you can see with absolutely clarity which way to go or what it is you need to do. When our thinking doesn't get in the way, our abilities become endless, even super-human. History is packed with miraculous stories of normal people doing the impossible.

There is a saying in martial arts: 'In all stillness there must be movement, and in all movement, there must be stillness.' If you have ever watched someone practising tai chi or qigong, or a Sufi dancer whirling around and around, you have a sense of what is meant by this saying. Regardless of what their limbs happen to be doing, you can see that they are moving from a still centre, like the calm in the eye of a storm. There is no exertion. It is a flow of effortless energy. It is stillness in action. We can all experience this when our mind is quiet and doesn't feel the need to get involved.

Think back to a time when you learnt a new sport or a new instrument. Remember the awkward, exaggerated movements as you desperately tried to remember the right sequence, timing and position you needed to be in for the most basic of moves. Everything felt odd and unnatural. Over time the movements started to become second nature; with less movement more happened and you could begin to feel a flow. You no longer had to think about what you were meant to be doing, you could do it off pat. Those who carried on reached another level, able to play around with the smallest nuances within every movement making flawless ad libs. You see it in top athletes and artists – that moment when all their practice comes together and they seem to transcend to a whole new dimension. Their focus is no longer on the action, they are completely free of any tension; everything on the mind has dissolved. It is as if *they* have dissolved. They are in an effortless flow, free of thought and not of their doing, channelling something more than human. It is the moment when anyone witnessing it knows something extraordinary is happening and the performer they are watching is performing from a different dimension. They are performing like immortals at a different level. The dancer is not just dancing exquisitely, they have become the dance, the musician the music, and the athlete achieves the impossible.

Even if you are not a top-level performer or athlete, we can all and probably have accessed the flow – a fleeting moment when we even surprise ourselves. The golf swing which barely makes a sound, the answer which comes out of nowhere, the moment when we transcend ourselves and perform out of our skin. When we get out of the way of ourselves, things beyond our imagination become possible. That said, do not expect that by simply going into stillness you are suddenly going to be able to produce a guitar solo like Prince or carry on where Stephen Hawking left off. You will need to have a few guitar lessons and attend a few physics lectures first.

# The Life Force

## A Subtle Power

*The quieter you become, the more you can hear.*
– Ram Dass

Stillness is not a destination. We are not the same as swimmers finally making it to dry land. Stillness is a portal, through which you discover all the dimensions which exist within each and every moment. Delicate nuances that unfold like flower petals are impossible to experience when we are constantly filling the silences and our eyes are only on the end goal. You start to see much more in less and you become aware of a subtle flowing energy in everything. This is not the obvious energy which we talk about when we say our battery levels are high or flat. It is a life force which flows through everything and connects us to the intricate web of life.

This is one of the first things which really caught my attention when I first met the Q'ero elders, Andean Shamans in Peru. They were normal folk living extraordinary lives, and much of that was because their simple lifestyle meant they were able to remain highly tuned and connected to everything around them. In the main, they were no different to me and you, except that they saw energy everywhere; everything was alive and had an effect on everything else. I can remember thinking how they were like walking metaphors of what it really means to be at one with everything. It's an inherent ability which fades when you have to contend with the fast pace of modern life. They are a perfect example of how less can be much more or, said another way, more can be infinitely less. Because the more crowded our lives become, the more removed and separate we become from a sense of belonging and connection with something far bigger and greater than the material world can ever offer.

We may not be able or wish to retreat to basic living on remote mountain tops for more than a couple of weeks, but we are now in the enviable position of being able to benefit from their knowledge and maybe tweak how we approach our own lives. Then we, too, can feel that same sense of connection, even if we live in a high-rise apartment in the middle of a city. Think back to the lake metaphor: the quieter and clearer our mind, the more we can see. When our minds are still and our opinion or experiences don't get in the way of what we are looking at, we, too, can perceive how this life force energy flows in everything.

This subtle energy sometimes gets a bad rap, but it is not good, bad or evil, but neutral like water. It is how we choose to use it which makes it either a positive or negative force. Think of it in the same way as pure water flowing in a mountain stream. The water remains pure while it moves in the flow. It is only when some rocks create little pockets and the flow gets disturbed and water becomes trapped that it starts to stagnate and become a breeding ground for disease. Like water, energy needs to move and we all innately know this. A small example is to think of it like walking into a room in a house where the energy feels 'off', stuffy and uninviting. The first thing we all do is open a window to let the air circulate and get the energy in the room moving again. The subtle energy which runs through our body is no different.

## It Is Second Nature

*If you want to find the secrets of the universe, think in terms of energy, frequency and vibration.*
– Nikola Tesla

When it comes to reading energy, it is absolutely true that it is a gift people are born with. But it is a mistake to think that it only applies to a select few. We can all do it, and we all *do* do it, and have done so since birth. Whether you are conscious of it or not, you are constantly tracking energy, whether you are watching the reaction on somebody's face or sensing the atmosphere when you walk into a room full of people. It is how we all interact with the world. Reading energy is really as much a part of being human as walking or talking. You might not literally see energy in the same way you can see heat over a tarmacked road in the midday sun, but you definitely perceive it. Because being able to read energy is a primal survival skill which kept our ancestors, well, at least the ones who were OK at it, out of mortal danger. The better you know how to read a situation, the better your chances of living, and when you are reading a situation, you are in effect reading the energy. You might not have the same finesse as a Shaman in the Amazon rainforest who sees everything as energy including you, or even your local reiki healer, but that is simply a matter of practice, training and curiosity.

Being able to read energy only helps us if we consciously take in what it is that we are reading and responding to. Otherwise it is as useful as the information sitting in a book high on a bookshelf. How we react to the different vibrations in ourselves as well as our environment is a case in point. We talk about the buzz of a city and the calm of the countryside, not to be poetic but because we literally feel it in our bodies. Imagine for a moment sitting by a picturesque still lake somewhere in the Alps enveloped by the gentle sounds of nature, and now imagine being crammed in the mosh pit at a gig next to giant speakers with the music not so much enveloping you as blasting through you. The effect each will have on not just our bodies but our entire system is obviously going to be very different. The soothing energy from sitting quietly by the lake is going to have a flatter vibration in comparison with the frenetic, spiky vibration of a high-energy gig. As much fun as the electric atmosphere is while you are at the concert, you want to be able to 'come down' afterwards and quickly find your equilibrium again.

We can all cope with a wide range of different vibration levels for certain amounts of time, some out of practice, some because certain vibrations suit our systems; but in just the same way we might like different music or like to wear different colours, we vary in sensitivity when it comes to the energy around us – we all respond differently to different vibrations. Some people come alive surrounded by a crowd, while others can do a bit and then need to escape to a sanctuary in the way you might from a sandstorm. One is not better than the other; it is simply knowing what works for you, so that when you fall out of balance you can find your own equilibrium. Realising that what suits somebody else may not suit you is key. As soon as you start to experience symptoms of unease, this is your personal red alert system warning you that you are doing more than you can manage and to back off. The first step is to slow down and simplify – metaphorically moving out of the mosh pit to recuperate by the still lake. Pare everything back in your life to the bare essentials so that you have room to rest, review and recalibrate.

Our natural understanding of energy is like a sixth sense. We might not be able to explain it, or we may just feel stupid admitting to it, but to various extents we all feel it. A primal part of us, perhaps unconsciously, judges whether a situation is safe or whether we need to be on alert for potential danger and we do this by reading the energy. Next time you walk into a room, take a moment and see what you notice. Ask yourself what it feels like. Try to avoid using your logical brain and let your instincts guide you. Anyone who is a success in business does this automatically. It is an essential part of making a successful negotiation, managing a team's dynamics or surviving a power play in the boardroom. Every salesperson is constantly reading the little energy nuances which give the green light to go for the close.

It might not be easy to see how we all hold and manipulate the energy in our everyday life, but really it is just a more subtle version of what every performer does on stage. Take a moment and think back to the best gig, concert, show or festival you have ever been to. Why was it so memorable? What was the energy like? Why was the artist's performance so good? Did they have the audience in the palm of their hand? How did they do that? Was the atmosphere electric? Mesmerising? Was it an experience unlike any other? If so, why? Again, try not to revert back to your intellect when you answer these questions. Be like the medicine men and women in the Amazon and see it all as energy.

One of the things that makes a performer stand out is their ability to work the energy in the room. However, when a performance doesn't take off it is like a spark plug continually misfiring. It can be the same performer doing the same show, exactly the same way, the only difference is the energy just doesn't flow between them and their audience. It happens to all of us. An awkward conversation, even with a close friend, where everything you say is off the beat and seems to come out wrong. It's like a vibrational mismatch. Meet one friend for coffee and you come away feeling drained like every last drop of energy has been sucked out of you, meet another and you come away buzzing with a spring in your step.

## How to move heavy energy

We all, on occasion, can be the energy vampire or the invigorator. It is not necessarily anyone's fault, but there are a couple of easy, seemingly innocuous exercises you can do when your energy feels like a weight dragging you down. The first is as simple as standing up and literally shaking it off in the same way you might jig about when you are really cold. Then, using your hands, brush your body as if you are removing dust from your clothes right down to your feet. Also brush the back of your head and, as much as you can, your back. It will have an effect.

The second is for when you are in the situation and you can't escape having to face someone else's energy head-on. This is a powerful on-the-spot visualisation you can do to avoid being affected by their outburst, regardless of whether it is raging, draining, spiky, frenetic or suffocating. Visualise whatever words they are saying and the emotions they are exuding as energy coming from them towards you, like the light trails you see in night photos of traffic or a fireworks display. In the same way you would dodge a flamethrower, or a bucket of water, or a punch, imagine doing the smallest of swerves to one side to let all their energy pass by you without touching you. If you are in an argument, this will help you to keep a clear head and not get swept up into an energy storm.

## Reading Between the Lines

*Kind words can be short and easy to speak, but their echoes are truly endless.*
– Mother Teresa

Energy will spark life and feed whatever we direct it towards, which is why setting intentions is so powerful. Wherever you put your focus, that is where your energy will go. When we set an 'intention' we are concentrating all our attention in one direction. The more we feed an idea with our thoughts, the more energy we give it. The more energy we give anything, the more life we give it, and so, by definition, the more it will grow. We don't even need to stock up or cultivate the energy because all the energy we can ever need is always readily available. All we need to do is decide where we want to focus it.

Imagine watering a garden. You do not need to create the water that comes out of the hose. You simply turn on the water and point the hose. The plants are just like our intentions and the hose is our focus. The ones you water have a chance at life; the ones you ignore don't. Just like the water coming out of the hose, energy doesn't judge where you direct it – it will go where you send it. Therefore, when you dwell on a toxic thought or a disparaging idea, you are giving it life. It is tantamount to watering weeds. Setting an intention is not the same as saying positive affirmations. Unless you put an intention behind an affirmation it is much the same as watering barren soil and willing flowers to grow.

The better we understand energy and how to balance it, the more it becomes obvious how we all at times disturb it. As nice as it would be to assume that we all go about our lives with hearts continually overflowing with compassion, we are all capable of behaving like a sorcerer and purposely causing friction and messing with the flow. It may seem small and insignificant, but the chances are that at some point in your life you have dished out a few dirty looks or said something you knew would really hurt somebody, because in the moment you wanted them to suffer. The chances are you also will have been on the receiving end and so you know that when a dirty look or a comment lands, it can hit like a sucker punch and floor you. It's normal. However, our actions have a direct effect on our bodies which can continue to hold the energy long after the look or comment was made. If you want to have an experience of this, try the following exercise with a friend.

Ask your friend to stand with their arms outstretched in front of them, their hands clasped and their two index fingers pointing out. Then, using the palm of one of your hands, gently push down on their clasped hands and test their resistance. It will be unlikely that they budge. Now tell them to close their eyes and to think of the saddest memory they have from their own lives. Tell them to focus their full attention on the event. Give them a moment to really engage, then again, using gentle pressure, see how easily you can push their arms down. Now do the same exercise but tell your friend to think of one of their happiest experiences ever and ask them again to hold the memory in their minds. Then, using the same pressure, push down on their arms. Get them to do the same exercise on you. The physical effects our thoughts have on us has to be experienced to be believed.

In today's world we talk so much that words can become a little like white noise. But words hold energy and the old saying, 'Sticks and stones may break my bones, but words will never hurt me' is completely inaccurate. Words are not 'just' words; they have an immeasurable power, particularly the ones we tell ourselves. A broken bone will mend, but words used as a weapon are drip-drip poison, which can continue working throughout an entire lifetime. We know this and still we can be really careless with how we use them. As we discussed in Step Two (page 57), each of us has a Shadow which holds the memory of words and tones that can trigger violent visceral effects in us. Words do not simply explain an emotion, they also create them. Words make you squirm, blush, scared or furious. A gifted narrator carefully picks their words to play with the energy in a story and hold their audience's attention. They understand words the way a composer understands music. Great speeches in history are examples of the electric power of well-chosen words and how they can galvanise an individual, a group, a crowd or a nation.

We need words to explain our feelings. However, unless you

are a wordsmith, it can be hard to find the right ones to express experiences we might all have, but still not necessarily feel in exactly the same way. So, we end up reducing a wealth of feelings down to one word, one to which we then all apply our own understanding. But you and I may have a very different physical experience of what it is to be terrified, depressed, exhilarated or off-the-charts happy. This doesn't really matter when it is a good feeling, but it does when it is a feeling we are struggling with and that we want to shift. We can talk about an emotion or a feeling, we can analyse why it came about, but sometimes it is easier and quicker to strip it right back to how the feeling is as an energy, and where and how it sits in our body, than relying on a word.

The following exercise is a slight variation to a trick I was taught by a medicine man if a vision turns bad. His response was simple – blow on it as if you were blowing smoke away from you.

## Imaginative healing

When you talk about feeling anxious, ask yourself how you literally feel. How you react to anxiety and how I react to anxiety may be very different. What happens to you physically when you are anxious? Does your stomach feel jittery, like a can of cola after it has been chucked around for a while, or does it feel like a void? How does your body 'do' anxiety? Stop for a moment, close your eyes and allow yourself to physically experience what happens to you when you become anxious. Imagine drawing the sensation with coloured pens so even a five-year-old child might get an idea of what you go through.

- What would you draw? A solid block of colour or a mesh of squiggles?
- What colours would you use?
- If you were to give it a temperature, would it be hot or cold?
- What would its texture be?
- Does the energy move around or is it stagnant?

Once you have a clear sense of the feeling and where it is in your body, using your imagination to picture the emotion, start breathing into it. If you have imagined that you have a sadness which sits in your stomach like a black rock, see your breath diluting the image you have in your mind's eye. With each breath, see the black rock turning grey and then white, and the rock starting to break up until it is just dust. Keep breathing into it until it has vaporised completely and then experience how it feels when there is nothing there to obstruct your natural energy flow.

## Good Vibes

*Do you know that our soul is composed of harmony?*
– Leonardo da Vinci

Another effective way to change or move energy when we feel down and out of our natural flow is with sound. Various versions of sound therapy have been used for thousands of years. The father of modern medicine, Hippocrates, used music to soothe nerves, settle mania and restore a harmony in his patients struggling with mental dis-ease. Plato described music as being the soul's medicine. Shamans throughout the world still use primal sound as a holistic healing tool because it is so effective at rebalancing our whole system.

Sound is made up of vibrations and so it is perfect for dissolving energy blocks or changing the energy completely. As I mentioned earlier, the medicine man I worked with in the Amazon was never interested in somebody's story, he couldn't even feign interest when they insisted on sharing it. He read their energy. He went to work in his medicine plant healing ceremonies where he could see exactly where a person's energy was blocked. He dispersed the energy through singing his personal icaros (sacred songs) and high-pitch whistling. His sole objective was to restore and rebalance the energy flow as if removing rocks from a stream. When I first worked with him, I wanted to understand the words he was singing, but it soon became clear to me that it was not *what* he was singing but *how* he was singing. The finesse of the vibrato at the end of each note was key, dispersing or expanding the energy, directing each person's experiences depending on their needs.

You do not have to be a Shaman or an ancient Greek philosopher to know the power of sound. We all naturally use it, humming when we are scared or nervous, whistling when we feel upbeat. Every parent naturally knows to sing a soft lullaby to soothe the senses of their baby and help it to feel safe. The one thing we all have access to is music. A simple mood-changer if you don't have a medicine man or sound therapist to hand is to put on a pair of headphones and play whatever music matches how you want to feel. It can lift or settle energy in seconds. If you are looking to raise your vibration, put on whatever tune makes you get up and dance. If you need to unwind or calm an anxious moment, have a music bath. Lie on the floor in a starfish position and play some natural sounds or classical music and let the music wash over you. Let the music completely consume you. It is important the music has no words so the mind has nothing to focus on and can completely relax. If you have ever stood by a speaker at a gig or in a club, you will know how sound can vibrate through your body. A music bath isn't dissimilar; it is just soothing rather than invigorating.

Then there is singing – one of the most powerful inbuilt healing tools we all have. If you like the idea of singing, really singing, I mean opening your lungs and singing with abandon, but you feel intimidated and not sure your local choir will value your commitment alone, then the ancient art of chanting is for you. Kirtan chanting is an Indian tradition which involves a call and response between the leader and the audience. It is like a conversation and it is perfect for everyone who wants to open their lungs, free of the fear of being out of tune. It is incredibly healing on many levels. The chants are healing in themselves, the sense of community is good for the soul and really allowing your voice to open without a sense of embarrassment or shyness is liberating. Chanting changes the vibration in your body which can help with everything from detox to depression, but above all else it is great fun.

If your local community has yet to form a chanting circle, you can get similar benefits from a humming meditation or a more traditional Om meditation.

## Humming meditation

You can do a humming meditation on your own, but if you have the opportunity to do this meditation in a group or even with just one other person, do so, as more people humming creates a continuous harmonic sound which is powerful.

- Sit in a relaxed position with your eyes closed and lips lightly touching.
- Start humming on the first note which comes out. Loud enough that you and anyone close to you can hear it.
- Focus on the vibration the humming sound makes. You may first feel it around your lips and face, play with sending it into your chest and belly. I like to cup my hands over my ears as it helps me to get lost in the sound.
- After a while you may find the hum becomes natural and you can play with changing the pitch around to find what feels right.

This meditation is also effective in moving the energy in your body as, with practice, you can send the vibration the humming creates anywhere in the body. So, if your chest feels tight like a clamp, send the vibration there to help release the tension.

### Om meditation

A traditional version of this meditation is Udgeeth Pranayama, which uses the sacred syllable Om (pronounced 'Aum') in a continuous chant. When it comes to spiritual sounds, Om is without doubt the best known and is considered by many a primordial, cosmic sound. Om is an ancient symbol, first mentioned in the Vedas, the ancient Indian scriptures, which date back to 1200 BCE.

- If you can, sit on a cushion cross-legged or, if it is more comfortable for you, a chair. Comfort is key. Either way, make sure you are sitting upright with the sense that each of the vertebrae in your spine is like a neat pile of books, resting one on top of the other.

- Imagine an energy force coming up your back, out of the crown of your head into the sky, like a cord holding you up, and another energy coming down through the crown of your head, down the shoulders, like a Christmas tree shape, towards the ground. So, you feel the energy is holding you in position in a relaxed state and you don't actually need to force anything.

- Take a deep inhale through your nose, filling your belly and chest, and, as you allow a long, slow, gentle exhale, chant the Om syllable: Aaaaa as in awe, with the sound coming from the belly; Ooooo as in oo, with the sound coming from the chest; and Mmmm, as in when something is delicious, with lips slightly touching so you can feel a gentle vibration with the sound coming from the mouth.

- As you chant, let the three sounds merge together. Try to extend the exhale to fifteen seconds or more, and then let the Om be silent in your mind before you inhale again.

## Human Energy Maps

*There is a force in the universe, which, if we permit it, will flow through us and produce miraculous results.*
– Mahatma Gandhi

Most of us think of the energy in our body as 'ours'. A separate, personal stockpile which we can store, supplement or deplete much like a tank of petrol, depending on what we eat, how we sleep and how much we do. And yet we know that if we eat a big roast lunch, rather than giving us a burst of energy it leaves us incapacitated in front of the TV, barely able to keep our eyes open. Whereas if we take up some form of regular exercise, rather than depleting our energy hoard we end up with more. Energy is not a commodity, it is a flow, and like a stream it can get clogged up and blocked, but when it is running freely it is limitless in supply. This subtle energy is the life force which runs through all of us and which we pay little attention to nowadays, but it holds a key to our well-being, mind, body and spirit.

Ancient China and India focused on how this life force flows through us with the same intensity as our doctors focus on our blood. This life force energy goes by many different names. In Chinese medicine it is called 'chi' or 'qi', yogis call it 'prana' and Shamans call it 'spirit'. Just as blood runs through a map of veins, this life force runs through energy channels called meridians in Traditional Chinese Medicine and nadis in the yoga texts. You may well have heard of the seven main chakras – the main energy junctions which start at the base of your spine and go up to the crown of your head. The Shamans also work with a chakra just above the head, where your halo might be. Way back when, the focus was much more on trying to prevent illness rather than trying to cure it. The doctor was paid to keep you well, which they did by keeping their patients' energy flowing by using diet, herbs, pressure point treatments and exercise. Some of the practices we are once more adopting today, like acupuncture, fasting, qigong and, of course, yoga, were devised by these doctors thousands of years ago to keep us healthy and our energy in flow.

The yoga asanas (postures) and qigong practices we do today to keep fit were developed not as random exercises, but from intricate studies focused specifically to keep the life force energy flow from being disturbed by any blockages, because the ancient doctors understood that this is what leads to disease. If you look at a yogi who has been practising for years, their body is incredibly strong but also supple. This energy flow is not a metaphor, it is very real. Watch a Shaolin monk cultivating such a strong chi flow that they can have cement blocks smashed on their stomachs or broken over an arm and it becomes patently obvious that it is not simply theory.

Understanding and knowing how to work with this life force is the source of our mental, physical and spiritual well-being. If you want to have a similar sensation of moving this life force energy, but you don't want to use your bare hands to break through concrete to test your chi, there are plenty of different practices to choose from. Yoga is without doubt the most popular and now a mainstream form of exercise in the West. Another is qigong, which is the exercise you may have seen practised particularly in China by groups, often older, in parks early in the morning. Both are powerful practices and not simply exercise as they are designed to bring the mind and body together using breath work.

Qigong and yoga are both moving meditations, but qigong is perhaps the easier of the two as the movements do not involve folding yourself into a human pretzel. This makes it easier to remember that the point of the practice is to find the stillness in the movement and not a bid to join an Olympic gymnastics team. Yoga is a philosophy which focuses on eight different fields, and the postures we all know so well are but one part. Pranayama is another.

Pranayama may be lesser known in the Western world, but all the traditional yogis I have met advocate that it is an essential part of their practice. Pranayama is the study on how to use conscious breathing exercises to work with the life force energy in your system. Its benefits and importance are innumerable. One of the first exercises you learn is alternate breathing which detoxifies the main channels of energy and is excellent for lowering stress levels.

## Alternate breathing

- Sit cross-legged on a cushion or, if you prefer, a chair, with your back relaxed but straight. Think of the pile of books (see page 184). Close your eyes and take a couple of slow, deep breaths to settle.
- Now, bring your right hand up to your face and place your right thumb on the side of the right nostril so it closes, and inhale through the left nostril.
- Then, close the left nostril with your ring finger, open your right nostril and exhale.
- Inhale through the right nostril, close the right nostril with your thumb and open your left nostril to exhale. This is one round.
- If this is your first time, do five rounds and focus on keeping the length of inhale and exhale the same. If your stress levels are high, do this exercise daily.

## Moving chi meditation

A basic qigong exercise to get a sense of the vital energy in and around your body is as follows:

- Stand with your legs hip-distance apart, your knees slightly bent. Let your back relax without slumping, soften your gaze, and let your breathing become natural and unforced.

- Bring your hands a little in front of your chest, fingers pointing up, palms not quite touching.

- Very very slowly, separate your palms. Move your hands, palms still facing each other, away and then slowly together again. Just as if you were playing an accordion or, if it is simpler, think of a tight rubber band around your hands so you have the sense of a resistance.

- Keep slowly moving your palms apart and then close together so you can feel in your hands something that feels like a ball of compressed air between them. This is chi. You may start to notice a dot in the middle of each palm begin to feel tingly and warm, and a magnetic feeling between the palms getting stronger. In qigong this is known as the 'Lao Gong' point – it is in the middle of the palm where the tip of your middle finger would touch if you were to make a fist.

- Keep a sense of the invisible ball between your palms and now play around a little. See if you can maintain the sensation if you make the tennis ball as big as a beach ball. As you bring the palms together, can you feel a resistance? If you are struggling to find the sensation, rub your palms vigorously together and try again.

The Lao Gong point is an important chi point in Chinese medicine which is used by hands-on energy healers. It is a significant energy gate on the heart master channel and is an excellent point to use for self-healing. As soon as you feel the chi flow in your hands, you can press on one Lao Gong point with the opposite thumb to help alleviate and support you in anxious moments. But, more importantly, you are experiencing the subtle energy flow. This is also another way of coming back into the body when your thoughts have taken you hostage. Sit still and focus on feeling the energy in your body; the pulse is your unique rhythm. This is the life force flowing through you.

# It's In Our Nature

## We Are the Land

*Humankind has not woven the web of life. We are but one
thread within it. Whatever we do to the web, we do to
ourselves. All things are bound together. All things connect.*
– Chief Seattle

For a Shaman, nature is alive. They see life in everything, not just
in trees and plants, but in the rivers, the mountains and the ground
we walk on. They respectfully refer to nature as Mother Earth
or Pachamama, because she is our life-giver who provides all of
us with everything we need, and they consider it their responsibility to look after her and her needs in turn. They are conscious
that we are not just part of nature, we are nature. We are inter-
dependent with the living world around us. The air you are
breathing into your body right now has come to you from faraway
mountains, rivers, trees, flowers and seas, and the air you exhale
you make feeds the mountains, the rivers, the trees, the flowers,
the seas, along with all the sentient beings. We are all part of a
magnificent web.

The speed of modern life means that at times we may feel far removed from everything and cut off from any supposedly magnificent web. But whether we are conscious of it or not, we are never alone or separate, even if over the centuries we have found more and more ways to shut nature out. This 'progress' has meant we don't have to spend our lives contending with nature's challenges, living at the mercy of the elements or contesting our cave with a territorial bear or snake. We have found ways to survive without ever really having to have any regular contact with nature at all. With thanks to modern advancements, most of us in the West have food in our fridge, water on tap, a cabinet full of medicine, which means we get to live longer lives and in considerable comfort. But that doesn't mean they are happier lives. The flip side of our increasingly sophisticated lifestyles is that, as we become more and more removed from the natural world, we are losing our sense of connection with one of the most powerful healers there is. Nature feeds not just our body, but our mind and our soul. Nature can calm an overstimulated mind, revitalise us when we lack lustre and be a sanctuary when we need solace.

Our distant ancestors did not have our creature comforts or our lifespan, but the flip side for them was they reaped some of the benefits we have lost. They had no choice but to get up and go to bed with the sun, so they never had to worry about their circadian rhythms (body clock) getting out of sync and causing havoc with their sleep patterns. They had a proper chance to destress every evening in front of a fire. Their lives were simple and immediate, and they had a deep connection with nature. They had to – their survival depended on remaining in harmony with her.

We might be more removed from nature than our ancestors, but that is not to say we don't love her or innately know that she holds an antidote to the hustle and bustle of modern life. Invariably when we set off on holiday, it is to some aspect of it, be it a sun-soaked beach or a snowy ski slope. Perhaps it is because nature runs in our blood that we feel so at peace when we are in it. It is where we retreat to when we need to relax, recharge and get ready to face the world again.

The main difference between us and our ancestors is that nature has become more of a wonderful backdrop or a canvas against which we live our lives rather than an ongoing live interaction. We love it and admire it, but few of us are engaged or in tune with it. We might go to watch wildlife in its natural habitat, hike in mountains or dive in coral reefs, but we do so as a visitor or an observer as if it is something apart from us.

Nature is spirituality in a nutshell and being in it is about as spiritual as you can get because it is an experience. It encapsulates balance, flow and a sense of connection – the same life force which flows through us, flows through nature. You don't need to read any sacred teachings, it is not something which needs to be intellectually understood. It requires no need for words of explanation or analysis. A core aspect of developing our Spiritual Intelligence is redeveloping a relationship with nature a little more like the one our ancestors had. Rebuilding a sense of connection with the living world around us so we can consciously feel part of something much greater than ourselves. This doesn't mean we have to up sticks, forgo our worldly goods and return to living in the wild. Unlike our ancestors, we can reap the benefits of both worlds. All we need to do is bring nature back to the forefront and stop long enough to really engage with it.

## Unplug and Reconnect

*One touch of nature makes the whole world kin.*

– William Shakespeare

A successful young businessman decided to take a couple of days out from his busy schedule and fly to the most beautiful place he knew to get away from it all. Jogging that evening by the mouth of a river he stopped in his tracks to admire possibly the most beautiful sunset he had ever seen. He heard a voice near him: 'Nature's gift!' The young man looked over to where the voice had come from to see an old man fishing close by also admiring the sun setting over the horizon. The young man nodded, looking back in awe at the bright red sun. After a while, the young man regained himself and took in the old man with not a care in the world sitting in paradise. Pointing to the fish by the old man's side, he complimented him on a successful day's fishing. The old man smiled and invited the young man to join him as he was about to make a fire and cook up the fish for dinner and he had more than plenty to share. Thrilled by the invitation, the young man sat with him as stars replaced the sun and the sea started to glisten in the moonlight.

As they sat there around the little fire not really talking, the young man piped up, 'This fish is delicious, you should bring out two fishing lines with you so you can catch even more.'

The old man replied, 'Why would I do that?'

At this, the young man's business mind started to kick in, 'Because then you could sell the extra fish in the market.'

'Why would I do that?'

'Because then with the money you make you can buy a small boat and a net and catch even more fish.'

'Why would I do that?'

'Because then with your profits you could employ your friends with boats to help you and catch even more so you have a successful small business.'

'Why would I do that?'

'Because this is how big business happens and if a little luck is on your side, you could end up a tycoon owning your own fleet of fishing trawlers and running a huge business.'

The old man looked totally nonplussed and again said, 'Why would I want to do that?'

The young man replied, 'Because then you can get other people to run your business so you can spend your days here in paradise just fishing.'

Lao Tzu, the father of Taoism, an ancient Chinese tradition, is quoted as saying, 'Nature does not hurry, yet everything is accomplished.' It's a reminder to all of us busy on life's hamster wheel that a definition of success which requires us to be always seeking more and continually forcing the pace may be a little skewed and one of the causes of mental distress. Given a chance, our screens and smartphones would constantly demand our attention so, for the sake of your well-being, it is important to take a moment every day to turn them off. Digitally detoxing, if only for an hour, is like removing the world from your shoulders. It is a chance to come out of your head and back to your senses. If you are someone who needs a purpose for doing something, and believe you do not have the time to stop and spend an hour in nature without your phone or music, you will be interested to know that doing this will expand your concentration span, and your problem-solving abilities will go up. It is like pressing the reset button for a tired mind.

The Japanese ancient practice of shinrin-yoku, which literally means 'forest bathing', re-emerged in the eighties as part of a national health programme to help people struggling with chronic fatigue, anxiety and deep depression from tech burnout. It became so popular that it is now a recognised national pastime. Studies showed it was a powerful antidote and just a couple of hours of being in a forest could reduce blood pressure, lower cortisol levels (our stress hormones) and leave practitioners feeling lighter, happier and with a deep sense of well-being. But forest bathing isn't going out for a walk; it is a moment to immerse yourself in nature using all the five senses. Instead of walking past the tree, it is watching the wildlife in the tree. It is a chance to slow right down and explore all the things you might normally walk past without noticing. It is the chance to experience the flowers, the birds in the trees and to listen to nature's orchestra of sounds – birds singing, twigs underfoot – and, if you wish to, hug a tree or two. Walking barefoot or sitting on the ground with your palms and the soles of your feet touching the earth doesn't just help us to feel grounded and back in our bodies when we have become lost in a world of thought, it will realign your circadian rhythms and, in doing so, your sleep patterns. Putting your hands in the soil releases microbes which are a natural antidepressant, stimulating the body's serotonin production making us happier and relaxed. Nature is a left- and right-brain paradise; it is both logical and random, which makes it as much a mathematician's dream as a poet's or artist's creative source. You can look for the symmetry in flower petals or the Fibonacci sequence on a pine cone or in the spiral on a snail's shell. When you slow down, you start to see and hear more. Ideally, you don't want to take anything with you – no phone, no music – but if your mind is too busy to settle, take a sketch pad. Few of us are lucky enough to have a forest on our doorstep, but the getting there is like a personal pilgrimage.

## Feeding the Mind, Body and Soul

*You and I are all as much continuous with the physical universe as a wave is continuous with the ocean. The ocean waves and the universe peoples.*

– Alan Watts

Nature is not a symbolic healer or a placebo, her medicine is real. Much of our modern medicine stems from plants and tree barks. Our ancestors learnt which plants healed often by watching which plants the animals turned to when they were sick. Both smart and logical, but it doesn't explain how the Native Americans knew to sit under a willow tree when they had a headache. The bark extract is the active ingredient in today's aspirin. Or how the Shamans in the Amazon rainforest worked out which plants would heal and which ones could kill. Not even trial and error can explain how they managed to put together combinations of different plants to cure specific ailments. Knowing which plants to choose from tens of thousands of different species and then finding the healing combination defies a rational explanation.

It suggests a profound connection which maybe we all had but most of us have now lost. But there is a road back to communing with nature and it can start with simply sitting under a tree. You might not find enlightenment or the next breakthrough in physics, but you will have a chance to boost both your mood and immune system from the antimicrobial essential oils that trees release. Trees are phenomenal healers – they can reduce blood pressure, a speeding heart rate, anxiety, confusion and depression. They can also help us in our bid to reconnect. So, when the weather is nice, take your meditation practice outside; copy the Buddha and find a tree to sit under. Sit with your back right up against the tree trunk and relax as you lean into the trunk, so the tree is holding you upright. Close your eyes and bring your attention to your back. Be still and look to feel the tree's energy. The quieter your mind and more open your body, the better your chances. An exercise a yogi in India taught me is to visualise each of the chakras which go up the spine like energy sockets plugging into the tree.

Developing our Spiritual Intelligence is about uniting our mind, body and spirit. Each is as important as the other. We need a healthy body so that the energy can flow, in exactly the same way we need our thoughts to flow and not get clogged. When the energy gets blocked – physically, mentally or spiritually – the balance is lost and there is the potential for dis-ease. What we eat affects what we think and how we feel, and it has a direct effect on our well-being. We all know the effects of too much coffee or a large dose of sugar and, when we feel depressed, our appetite is immediately affected. Every spiritual tradition advocates fasting, not as a means to make sure you are 'beach body ready' or to strip the joy out of life, but because it is an effective way to remove toxins and reset the energy flow for the mind, body and spirit.

## Mindful eating meditation

Food is medicine. It is also another way in which we remain connected. Once in a while, before you start eating, take a moment to track how the food got to your plate all the way back to its origins. Imagine the potato in rich soil, or the avocado hanging in its tree, or the fish swimming in the sea. The sunshine, rain clouds, wind and earth which helped them grow. As you take each mouthful, know you are feeding your body with that same sunshine, rain and earth.

## At Home with Nature

> *One of the first conditions of happiness is that the link*
> *between man and nature shall not be broken.*
> – Leo Tolstoy

Nature does not have to mean the vastness of the Himalayan mountain range or the expanse of a wide open sea, it can be a little garden the size of a postage stamp or simply looking up into the sky. If you are someone who cannot get out into nature as often as you would like, or at all, so long as you have access to a window you can still get lost in nature. Sky-gazing is a quick way to cut through a busy mind; for the mature, simply watching the clouds slowly pass, for children of all sizes, spotting animals in the clouds is a fun way to allow your mind to have a moment's relaxation and perhaps a reminder not to take life too seriously. When you spot a giant bunny rabbit in the clouds, maybe it is proof that even nature has a sense of humour.

## Energy spring clean

Allowing nature into your home with pets, plants and fresh air goes a long way to keeping a nice energy flowing, but it is good once in a while to give your home an energy spring clean. Throughout the ages, throughout the world, plants like sage, tobacco, cedar, sweetgrass and palo santo have been burnt to cleanse and protect homes. They are nature's antiseptics and all of them are excellent at dispersing any energy blocks. It is easy to do, but a word of warning, if you choose to use a sage bundle, I suggest you first use only a small amount – a whole bundle can be overpowering and may set off the smoke alarms.

Pick an aroma you like and, if none of them appeal to you, open all the windows and let nature cleanse your home for you. Whatever you choose to use, be it palo santo or white sage, please make sure it is from a sustainable source. Light a bundle or a stick (depending on what you use) and blow it out so it starts to smoke. Then go into each room and, using a large feather or your hand, push the smoke into all the corners of the room. While you are at it, you can use the smoke to cleanse away any stagnant energy on yourself as well. Pass the smoke around your body, front and back, under the arms, between the legs and under the feet. Unless you are using sage, which once lit will not go out, you will need to keep relighting the wood.

## How to use crystals

Another great way to change the energy in a home is with crystals and mineral stones. Both have been used as healing tools and to ward off dark energy since ancient times, and they are a perfect way to connect to nature from within your own home. Placed correctly, they can help keep the energy flowing and prevent pockets forming. Put celestine in your bedroom on your bedside table to calm and help you sleep or a fluorite on your desk to give you clarity. Whatever you feel about their properties, crystals and minerals are yet another example of nature's rich diversity.

I always carry a pocket stone with me – it is like carrying nature in your pocket. I have a bowl of small stones at home and each morning I pick one depending on my mood and what I feel I need. Sometimes it might be a stone someone has gifted me or one I have picked up from near a sacred site or a place in nature special to me. It can just as easily be one which caught my eye in a shop. If I need a little magic in my day, I might carry some labradorite as it shimmers like the Northern Lights; or if I feel off balance, I will take a jasper to ground me as it holds a lower and slower vibration. Unpolished stones are perfect for anxiety as they feel most like nature and are easier to connect with. Throughout the day I will find myself just holding it or playing with it in my hand. Holding a piece of nature is instantly calming.

If you find you are struggling or feel off-balance during your day for whatever reason, blow the energy into the stone and at the end of the day clean it by either putting it in the earth of a pot plant or in running water. Next time you are somewhere special pick a small stone to take with you. If you want to do it the Shamans' way, rather than grab and go, take a moment when you see one and quietly ask permission of the land. Then place the stone near your lips and blow an intention or gratitude with your breath into the stone. I can remember once being told that those really pretty stones that you might pick up only to find, when you look at them a while later, that they aren't quite as attractive as you first thought so you drop them back on the ground, are the stones' way of using you as a donkey to take them to a new place. Similarly, when you lose a pocket stone or leave it behind, do not fret – it has left you because you no longer need it anymore, and it is there to be picked up by someone who does.

## Lose yourself in nature meditation

This is a little visualisation you can do when you can't get outside and maybe feel alone or cut off and need to feel held.

- Lie down and close your eyes.
- Take a few deep breaths and, on each exhale, let your body sink. Let the back of your head melt and your shoulders drop.
- Now, using your imagination, take yourself to a place in nature, real or imagined, where you feel free. Use all your senses to be there now. See the landscape in your mind's eye, hear the noises of nature and the sounds of the wildlife. Remember how the air feels against your skin. Remember how your body feels when you are in this place in nature. Remember how your body feels when you feel free. Imagine lying back and just letting this place in nature hold you, just as a parent may hold a newborn baby.
- Allow yourself to surrender, to feel held with each exhale, letting your body sink deeper, totally relaxed, nothing for you to do but just be. Imagine becoming so immersed in this place in nature that you feel your body dissolving, your energy and the energy of the nature merging together. Let everything you are holding on to dissolve as you and nature become one. Let everything go.

- Enjoy the sense of being formless, enjoy the sense of merging with nature, of being one and the same with nature. Stay with this as long as you wish. Then, when you are ready, imagine your body starting to take form again, cleansed, refreshed and nourished by this place in nature.

- Take a moment to feel that sense of freedom wash through the whole of your body so you can carry it with you, and you can feel it wherever you are, whenever you want.

## Humble Gratitude

*Only when the last tree has died and the last river has been poisoned and the last fish been caught will we realise we cannot eat money.*

– Cree Native American proverb

We all have plenty in our lives to be grateful for, nature being at the top of any list. Gratitude goes hand in hand with humility. Both are potent healers because they take us out of ourselves and open us up to something bigger than ourselves and our own ideas of our rights and importance. It is humbling to realise that, although we are an important part of nature, we are not that important a part. The natural world will continue to survive and flourish without us, but we, on the other hand, cannot exist without it. The word humble comes from the Latin word 'humus', which means earth. When we are humble it is a reminder that we are all of humble origins and it is a good way to stay grounded. It is really easy to focus on all the things that are not right about our lives and forget all the things that are. But when we do and feel grateful for them, it comes with some surprising benefits. Studies in positive psychology show that feeling grateful raises both dopamine and serotonin levels in the brain. A dopamine surge is like a natural high – it helps us feel better about ourselves. It also makes us happier and more optimistic about our life and show more empathy towards others. A good practice is each morning to list in your mind three things in your life you are truly grateful for. It may be an ability, a job, or it may be a person you have in your life. In the evening before you roll over to go to sleep, take a moment to remember three things in the day you are grateful for. It is a good way to catch the sweet moments in a day which are so easy to shoot past.

Remembering to show gratitude for nature in real time and not just in theory was one of the first lessons I had early on in my spiritual training with the Q'ero elders. One time on a difficult hike, due to a mixture of midday sun, some steep switchbacks up a never-ending mountain plus a general lack of fitness, I found myself struggling. As I started to trail the small group I was with, the oldest elder noticed I wasn't faring too well and stopped to wait for me. He told me to stop seeing the mountain as something I needed to overcome or conquer and that the mountain was not in the way of my destination. He gave me a kintu (prayer leaf bundle – see page 140) and told me to blow in my gratitude to the mountain for taking me where I wanted to go. We continued walking at a pace no faster than a stroll looking around thanking absolutely everything. He insisted on a rhythm of thanking the mountain, then the flowers we were walking past, the sky, the birds, the view. I can remember being a little annoyed and thinking it was silly, but I liked him, so I did what he told me. I copied everything he told me to say and I quickly started to really enjoy it. It definitely beat staring at the ground willing my dusty shoes to keep moving. As soon as he felt I had got the hang of it, he took a wooden flute out of his poncho and started to play random notes with no noticeable tune to accompany all my gratitudes. A two-hour climb somehow disappeared in a moment and, before I knew it, we had arrived at one of the then lesser known Inca ruins, Choquequirao. Instead of a predictably filthy mood, I was laughing and, bizarrely, no longer tired.

## Ayni Despacho ceremony

The Andean Shamans have a beautiful ceremony of gratitude called an Ayni Despacho. 'Despacho' in Quechua, their mother tongue, means to give back and 'Ayni', roughly translated, means right relationship or balance. It is an offering of gratitude to nature for all the things she has given us which we often take for granted. Each ingredient of the despacho symbolically represents a different element and is carefully placed to create a beautiful mandala. The despacho is then folded up in the same way you would wrap a present. As with any ceremony, the most important element is our intention. There is no right or wrong, it is important to find your own way to make it special and meaningful for you. Take your time over it – this isn't a quick nod of thanks, but a moment for you to come back to yourself and be grateful for the different things in your life.

You will need a sheet of wrapping paper. Fold it into three one way, open it back up and then fold into three the other way, so when you open it back up the folds will have made nine squares. The despacho is made on the one in the centre. Have all the things you would like to put in the despacho ready so you can enjoy creating it (they do need to be natural items that will in time decompose). As for what to put in, let your imagination lead you. Pick different ingredients to symbolically represent all the ways you depend on nature. The bottom layer might be grains and nuts from your kitchen cupboard to represent sustenance, corn to represent the abundance of food the earth grows, fruit or sugar to represent the sweetness of life, herbs for healing, spices for the weather; maybe add some soil, or some sand if you live near the sea. Wine and chocolate are all included in a traditional despacho. The upper layers may be flower petals and kintus each for different things that you are grateful for. Take a moment with each one to blow your thank you before placing it in the mandala. The Q'ero also use carnation flowers, a white one to represent the mountains and a red one to represent the earth. When you feel you have finished, fold the paper over the mandala and tie it with string. Place one more kintu on the outside of the parcel to represent all the prayers or wishes you might have forgotten to include. At the end of the ceremony, the despacho can be burnt or offered to a river of water to be digested by Pachamama, Mother Earth.

## Awe

*There are two ways to live your life. One is as though nothing is a miracle. The other is as though everything is a miracle.*

– Albert Einstein

Another beautiful side to humility is a sense of wonder; a humble realisation of how small our individual lives are within the enormity of the cosmos. Awe is a feeling which makes us come out of our individual internal worlds and move our focus from our own immediate needs or struggles to feeling a part of something much greater than ourselves. Nature continually offers us moments of 'stop in your tracks', jaw-dropping awe. Stand under a giant Sequoia tree, visit Antarctica, walk in a rainforest or scuba dive in any ocean and you will likely feel awe. But perhaps the ultimate 'awe' is a full moon or the immensity of a night sky covered with a blanket of stars on a clear night. It is hard to see either and not have a sense of awe. Looking into the stillness of the night sky's inky black infinity is the quickest way to iron out a furrowed brow. It creates a space in a busy mind for the imagination. The ego dissolves as the realisation dawns that we are all part of something magnificent.

When life is hard for whatever reason, if you can, just look up into the night sky and remember that you are looking up at the same stars as the great spiritual teachers and legends of the past did, and they are the same stars our children's children will one day look up and see too. We are the link which connects the two.

# Soul Talk

## Stepping Into Our Power

*The summit of happiness is reached when a person is ready to be what he is.*

– Erasmus

The final reconnection involves trusting some of the deeper dimensions within us that we rarely give the light of day, because as intriguing as they may be, we don't have confidence in them. At least, we don't feel we can completely rely on them in the same way we depend on our rational mind and it is hard to consider that they have any real value. But these dimensions are the missing jigsaw pieces, because our life can never truly feel complete until we are prepared to listen to our intuition, pay attention to our dreams and make use of our imagination. These jigsaw pieces form a different type of intelligence to our logical brain, but are every bit as important. See it as the icing on the cake, because it is this intelligence which not only gives purpose and meaning to life but gives it its magic.

Our intuition, imagination and dreams connect us to our soul

– our own personal sage, a knowing voice which we hear in our heart of hearts, or somewhere deep in our gut. It is our soul which gives us the courage and conviction to follow our passions and live life in a way that is right for us. It is our soul which gives life its depth and flavour. So, when life continues to feel boring and empty regardless of how much stuff we buy or ways we find to distract ourselves, it points to a soul disconnect. And when we live life without soul, it always feels like something deep down is missing; we never really feel whole. As we have seen, the language of the soul is art, music, ritual and ceremony. It is the part of us that a song or guitar solo touches, or the work of art stops us in our tracks. It is the profound place we go to in the silence of a ceremony. It is in the delight of a belly laugh.

## We Can Be Heroes

*We must let go of the life we have planned, so as to accept the one that is waiting for us.*
– Joseph Campbell

When we think of life thousands of years ago and our ancestors sitting around fires, it is easy to assume that their levels of intelligence would be no match to ours now, regardless of the fact that those ancestors include the great Greek philosophers, mathematicians, inventors and playwrights that underpin the modern world. We can forget that our fundamental concerns today were their concerns as well and, like us, one of the biggest was all the complexities of being human.

Some of the greatest insights on the human condition can be

found in ancient mythology. It is easy to be dismissive about myths and reduce them to no more than a collection of entertaining stories from a bygone era. It might be hard to fathom how epic tales of heroes overcoming seemingly insurmountable obstacles (with the odd capricious god, giant or creature thrown in for good measure) can have any real bearing in today's world. However wise their insights may have been then, they can hardly be relevant or a match for our knowledge today, and yet they are.

Because the great myths are not just primitive bedtime stories to tell your children, they are timeless life maps and valuable teaching tools which guide us through the rip currents of human nature like wise old mentors helping us make sense of our lives. They express a wisdom that demystifies the meaning of life and unites us all in a common origin, a collective unconscious, irrespective of where we were born or what culture we were brought up in. Mythology tells the story of us. The ancient myths are universal maps which act like a compass to tell us where we are in our own personal journey. They are our ancestors showing us, through the power of story, some of life's twists and turns and how to navigate them and get through the main stages of life.

At the heart of the myth is the 'hero's journey'. This is a term coined by the late Joseph Campbell who realised that the stages the protagonists have to go through – in every myth from the Knights of the Round Table to a Jedi Master in *Star Wars* – are the same stages we all face. The hero in the myth represents each of us in our own epic tale, which is why the stages of the hero's journey resonate with all of us, young and old. It is a symbolic journey which shows how each of our lives is like an adventure packed with a series of seemingly insurmountable challenges, which force us to dig deep and find inner qualities we didn't know were there. It is why we find ourselves willing on an animated lion cub and rejoicing when it finds an inner resolve not to give up and become a victim of its circumstance, and in the process becomes a hero.

These stories are food for the soul because the symbolism in myths gets underneath the skin of everyday life and talks directly to a deeper dimension within us. It is the call to adventure when we realise we are not living life fully. It is the little voice inside us which keeps telling us that there is more to life than the one we are living and coaxes us to make a change. This doesn't mean we all have to take up skydiving, it is simply a nudge to make sure we are living whatever our choice of life is, fully.

These ancient stories not only open our vision and prick our imagination, but they can awaken a deeper passion for life in us. They evoke a sense of awe which allows us to transcend the minutiae of our daily lives and begin to experience the extraordinary within the ordinary. They trigger an impulse, a seed of potential in us, to see something bigger and to be something better.

Like metaphors, myths were never meant to be taken literally. They hold a truth which speaks directly to the part of us which responds to symbols rather than words, a truth which cannot be fully computed by our intellectual mind. When you take the myths literally, you lose the magic and you miss the message. Because the magic is not in the myth or the metaphor, it is in what it evokes in you. Myths give you a sense of the mystery of you as well as the mystery of life. Depending where each of us is in our own epic, we will draw from the hero's journey what we need. This doesn't necessarily correlate with our age. There are young people who, like the lion cub, have already learnt to dig deep and face their fears, and older people who have done their level best to avoid any challenge. It is never too late to face up to fears or emotions you never dared face before.

Ask yourself where you are in your own story:

- What are the challenges you would like to overcome?
- What are the dragons (emotions, not people) that are standing in your way?
- Ask yourself, 'Why not now?'

## Never Just a Dream

*The intuitive mind is a sacred gift and the rational mind is a faithful servant. We have created a society that honours the servant and has forgotten the gift.*
– Albert Einstein

Every night when our rational mind clocks off for the day and we become unconscious to the world, a space opens in the mental noise and our soul finally gets a chance at the microphone our intellect so loves to hog. The problem is that our soul doesn't speak the same language as our intellect. It prefers symbols and images to words, which means when it tries to communicate to us, normally in our dreams, it is not immediately obvious what exactly it is trying to say.

Symbols in a dream are random, bizarre and, at face value, don't seem to make any sense. We easily shrug them off as nothing more than momentarily fascinating or weirdly entertaining. More often than not we have forgotten them before we have scrambled out of bed to make a cup of coffee. Just because our dreams aren't straightforward though, it doesn't mean they are pointless gobble-dygook. Dismiss them as merely cobbled together colourful offcuts of yesterday's thoughts and you are cutting yourself off from a valuable source of wisdom. It is important to know how to interpret your night's entertainment.

Analysing dreams is something humans have done across every culture for thousands of years. Some, like Pharaoh with his cows, have prophetic dreams, but for most of us our dreams give us a heads-up to any repressed fears or feelings which might still be hiding out in our unconscious.

Dreams can also offer us direction and be a powerful source of inspiration. When you consider that Einstein's theory of relativity, the periodic table, the discovery of DNA, the structure of the atom, insulin, Google and the sewing machine all came from dreams, then learning how to read your own dreams may suddenly hold more value.

First, though, there is the problem of remembering them. Regardless of how intense a dream may have been, often the moment you open your eyes it evaporates into nothing, which makes it of prime importance to have a reliable way of catching it. Trying to hold a dream in your head as you wake up is as precarious as holding bubbles, so you need to recap the dream while you are still in that half-sleep twilight zone, before you open your eyes. One way to do this is to link the key figures and places in a mnemonic sequence, then as soon as you open your eyes immediately get it down on to paper, even if it is half memories. As you write down the salient points, the chances are you will also capture other parts of the dream before they vanish. Writing may feel like the last thing you what to do when you wake up, but the likelihood of you remembering your dreams even in a memorable sequence isn't great, so a journal by your bed is essential if you want to analyse them. The more you write down your dreams, the more you will remember and you will start to recognise certain symbols and be able to notice recurring elements. It takes a bit of effort, but it is worth it because, although one dream might make no sense or not even be particularly interesting as a standalone, the message may well only become clear when you can see it as part of a sequence of dreams.

If you are reading this and thinking this is all great for those who *do* dream, starting a dream journal also works for anyone who is convinced they don't dream at all. Here is a quick two-step method to start recalling your dreams. Every night as you turn over to go to sleep you must set an intention to remember your dreams, just a short sentence like, 'I am going to remember the dreams I have tonight, when I wake up.' Then, as soon as you wake up in the morning, if you don't remember dreaming write on the top of a clean page in the journal 'no dream to report'. Do this every day and, within a few weeks, you will be recalling your dreams. The next stage on from recalling dreams is lucid dreaming, which allows you to consciously walk about your dream in real time, but that is only helpful once you have learnt how to decipher the symbols in a basic dream.

Just like in myths, there are lots of common symbols and themes in all our dreams. However, unlike myths, they do not hold a universal meaning. Dream analysis is not an objective science, so it is better not to rely on an online dream dictionary to help you decode, for example, what a frog in a dream might mean. Our dreams are deeply personal and remembering the emotions the images triggered in you is far more pertinent. If you dream of finding a little white dog on your doorstep waiting for you to come home, the dream is going to have a very different feeling for the person who grew up with a little white dog which used to sleep on their bed than the person who was terrorised by their neighbour's Jack Russell. Your soul isn't using its own well-thumbed copy of a dream dictionary to send you messages, it is encrypting your dreams using experiences and feelings towards different things which only you will truly understand. This is good news as it makes any analysis a lot easier.

When you have a vivid dream which doesn't make any sense, treat it in the same way as a myth or a metaphor and first ask yourself what feelings the whole dream evoked in you:

- Did you wake up feeling upbeat or unsettled?
- Was the dream set in a place which is familiar to you and, if so, how do you feel about that place?
- If it wasn't a specific place or one that you know, what was it like and how did you feel being in a place like that?
- Did you feel cautious or free?

Write down the answers in your journal. Then pick out each of the main characters in the dream and remember how in the dream you felt towards each of them. Sometimes people you know will pitch up – from good friends to people you occasionally see in the office to people from long ago in the past. What characteristics best describe these people in your eyes? If the lollypop lady who used to stand outside your nursery school turns up, ask yourself what you used to think of her when you were a child. Was she warm and compassionate or did she always tell you off for not paying attention crossing the road? Now you have to ask yourself, is the lollypop lady and all the other characters there to direct you towards something or are they all representing characteristics within you? Remember how you actually felt in the dream towards these people and any other characters and it may give you an insight into how you feel about those characteristics in you.

Now turn your attention to what happened in the dream. Unlike the symbols, actions can have universal meanings, so note if you were running in the dream, what you were running to or away from. Did someone die in the dream or, for that matter, did you die? If so, death in a dream does not mean you are foreseeing an imminent tragedy. When most of us see death in a dream, as with tarot cards, it tends to suggest a big change or transformation.

Do not worry if your dreams aren't jazz hand showstoppers. Mundane dreams can be just as revealing. Even those ones where it feels like your thoughts never actually switched off and your dream had you writing to-do lists and going through piles of office admin. There is a message there.

## Reading the Signs

> *Oracles reflect what you already know, they mirror the energy you're dealing with and help you navigate your world.*
> – Colette Baron-Reid

If you are not up for waiting for messages from your soul to make their way through in your dreams, there are methods where you can get some live feedback. Although few of us have the gift of the Oracle at Delphi or the know-how to read a bunch of bones, yarrow stalks or leaves, there are two highly effective tools we can all use regardless of whether you feel you are blessed with a gift or not.

The first is oracle cards. Working with oracle cards is a little like visiting a great living seer or guru for guidance and direction, only the guru happens to live deep within you. They are a brilliant way to get a conversation going with your soul and ask some direct questions. Oracle cards are also great at guiding us to see what we need in our life and how to reshape and re-evaluate different areas in our life. It might sound quite a lot of responsibility for a deck of picture cards, but the power is in what they touch in you, not the cards themselves. That is to say, as a deck of cards they do not wield any power or insights on their own, in just the same way a guitar doesn't play the blues on its own. It might be tempting to just pick a card without any real thought and read it at face value. You might be momentarily thrilled when you pick a 'good' card and, when you don't, quickly pick another one until you get the message you want, but it is unlikely to bring you any insights unless you stop for a moment and engage with it. Anytime you want to pick a card for guidance, pause. Let your mind go still, think of a question you want to ask, focus on it and then pick a card. Anyone who has had a reading from a specialist knows that, however brilliant the specialist is, not everything they say will resonate. Maybe the information you were given needed to perco-late over a period of time before it clicked with you, but there may have been points which just didn't touch at all and so we rightly disregard them. Working with oracle cards is visceral. You will know when something touches your soul and you need to maybe sit up and listen.

Another method which only requires a pen and a piece of paper is unconscious writing. Julia Cameron made this popular in her book *The Artist's Way*. It is giving your pen free rein with no concern for spelling, grammar, punctuation or whether it makes any sense. It is a method to help you slip past the barrier the conscious mind creates which can block us from sourcing inspiration from the deeper dimensions of you. You can either write for a certain number of pages or for a set amount of time, the only thing you need to do is keep writing once you've begun. Write about whatever is on your mind – thoughts, worries, ideas, dreams. It is an effective way to clear an overloaded mind, process emotions and let your imagination fly. The more often you do it the easier it will become to allow a flow which you end up being a witness to, rather than a part of. When you get proficient at allowing this flow you can write out a specific question at the top of the page and then, changing pens, let your soul answer it. It is like sitting in front of your very own guru. There is something magical about the process, particularly when you realise that the information is coming from within you and not somewhere over the rainbow. It may surprise you what comes up.

## Why Not Now?

*To see is to experience the world as it is, to remember is to experience the world as it was [. . .] to imagine is to experience the world as it isn't and has never been, but as it might be.*
– Daniel Gilbert

Do you remember when you were a child what you wanted to be when you grew up?

Whatever it was, you probably had no doubt in your mind that you would indeed one day be a fireman, ballerina, doctor or astronaut, and it was both fine and standard if the next day you said with equal conviction that you wanted to be a pilot, an Oompa Loompa or even a tractor. As a child, we knew our imagination as an infinite invisible world where everything was possible, we just had to think it. Cardboard boxes became great castles and it was considered perfectly normal to commune with flies and fairies and never leave the house without at least one toy. We were masters at creating something out of nothing.

Then school started, life became more serious and 'reality' took over. We learnt to pay attention, to not look out the window and we learnt that daydreaming was for the idle. As we grew up and conformed, so did our imagination, and a world of infinite possibilities was reduced to the real world of probabilities. Dreaming too big became foolish and we learnt how to quickly quash our aspirations before someone else did, and that it was easier and safer not to veer too far off the well-trodden path.

Obviously, once grown-up, the world full of dragons, unicorns and leprechauns guarding pots of gold no longer holds quite the same appeal, but our power to imagine is one of the greatest gifts we have. It is what gives us the power of creation. We need to be careful not to let our busy lives in the 'real world' squeeze out time to daydream, when we can just let our imagination fly.

There is little more magical or mysterious than the intangible and invisible world of the imagination. After all, where is it? Have you ever wondered how an idea that is way outside of your own learnt knowledge actually gets into your thoughts? How can it be possible to dream beyond the boundaries of your own finite knowledge? The imagination is elusive. It demands freedom to roam and it refuses to be at the beck and call of our rational mind. We can't put 'have a great idea' on our 'things to do list' or expect inspiration to pitch up on cue as soon as we sit down at our desk. The more you furrow your brow and try to imagine anything, the less chance you have of it taking flight. Then, out of the blue, apropos of nothing as you are taking the dishes out of the dishwasher and the answer to humanity pops into your head.

Ideas have an elusive cat-like quality to them, lingering just out of reach. They rarely come to our call. Ideas tend to respond to light and playfulness more than panicked desperation, mainly because they open the mind. A curious mind and a want to explore is catnip for our imagination and, although we might not be able to summon genius at will, the more we daydream and allow our imagination the freedom to wander, the more ideas will come to us.

In fact, our dreams are fundamentally important because only what we dream can become reality. Our imagination is where every idea and dream begins. It is the backbone of reality.

The modern world is proof. All its incredible advancements are built on ideas which were once imagined by individuals wondering 'What if?' But we all play a part in each discovery as how we live life forms a collective attitude of what is needed. This is the reality which forms the foundation from which future inventions can grow.

Each of us, every day, is dreaming our own reality with how we view the world. See the world as a dog-eat-dog dangerous place and that is what your world will be. See it as a community looking out for each other and that is what your world will be. The universe has a way of proving you right, possibly because you will behave according to your beliefs and so prove it to be true. How we are in the world is how the world becomes. You will notice only the scowls and not the smiles or vice versa. The reality is that they will all be mirroring you. Our choices collectively chart the course reality takes. We are all co-creating the world every day. It is remarkable to realise that if we are all responsible for how the world is and we don't like it, we have the power to change it, starting with ourselves. As the African proverb states, 'If you think you are too small to make a difference, try sleeping with a mosquito.'

This applies to our personal lives too. If your reality is not panning out the way you had hoped and you have become a victim of circumstance, you have the power to alter it and to create a new reality for yourself. We need to use our imagination to call in the life we do want.

The question is, what to call in? We can all reel off a long list of what we don't want in life, but aside from a few material goodies, we can't necessarily say what it is that we *do* want. This is because we rarely put any real detail into our dreams. We tend to talk in broad strokes. 'I want to be happy.' 'I want to be fulfilled.' 'I want to find my soul's purpose.' Wanting to be happy and have a fulfilled life is a great dream, but what does that actually look like to you? What exactly makes you happy? Have you ever stopped to really think about what you actually mean on a day-to-day detailed level?

Take a moment and get a piece of paper. At the top of the page write down what one of your dreams is. Let's take 'I want to be happy' as an example. Now write down everything that that means to you. You will notice that as you write down all your different points, the dream will start to unfold and not necessarily quite how you may have expected. You may be amazed that writing out the dream reveals to you things about your idea of happiness that you had never even registered. Once it feels like you have written the dream down in its entirety, look at what you need to do to bring it about right now, today! You might find that it is simply a matter of tweaking what you already have and doesn't actually involve the huge shift in direction that you might have been fearing. But perhaps the most important aspect of any dream is, does it have the potential to fulfil you? All dreams, however wonderful or virtuous, are completely pointless if you leave them dangling on a rainbow. It is not a matter of having an idea of a dream and then sitting back and hoping it is going to materialise of its own accord. All ideas have to be nurtured and fed until they are strong enough to make the journey from the invisible to the visible world. If your dream is important to you, why keep yourself waiting?

## Bring it Home

> *Our healing is not complete until we ourselves become healers.*
> – Alberto Villoldo

Regardless of where we come from, our upbringing, our culture or our lifestyle, we all want our lives to have at least some meaning to them. At some point we start to wonder what our life's meaning is and what is our soul's path. It is what draws many of us to spirituality. 'Soul's path' is another one of those great big state-ments which gets bandied around, but no one really quite knows what it means. It is safe to say that our purpose and our path are one and the same. If you are wondering, 'Where do I find mine?' or, 'How will I know if and when I am on it?', a soul's path is a way of living life which comes from following the things that you find important. There is no right or wrong path – it is personal to you. It isn't something bestowed upon you, nor do you have to pick one path and hope you have picked the right one. It comes out of you. That said, finding your soul's purpose or path is rarely clear from the outset.

The quickest way to find your purpose and have a meaningful life is to follow your interests and passions. If you are not sure what those are, ask yourself how you would live your life if you were completely free to do whatever you want. What would you fill your days doing if you had absolutely nothing to worry about? What would you like to learn more about if you had all the time in the world? Spend as much time as you can on these interests. As you do, new worlds will continue to reveal themselves. It may be several careers later when you realise there was a common thread running through all of them, each in turn taking you towards your soul's purpose. Let your curiosity guide you. As Joseph Campbell said, 'Follow your bliss and the universe will open doors where there were only walls.'

But it is worth noting that a soul's path does not equate to Easy Street, not in the sense of 'Phew, I've found it', sigh of relief, search over, the hard stuff is now behind you so you can relax. There would be nothing fulfilling about it if it did. It may turn out to be the hardest thing you have ever done and, at times, force you to dig deep and question whether it is indeed your path. The clue that it is, is when you realise that you couldn't dream of doing anything else. It may be tough and involve perseverance, but the tears will be from laughter. You will know for sure that it is your soul's path when it becomes something which serves others in some way as well as yourself. It is like coming home. It is the deep-rooted happiness His Holiness the Dalai Lama was referring to.

# Going Forward

*Always laugh when you can. It is cheap medicine.*
– Lord Byron

The power of all spiritual teachings and practices is they continue to unfold, so each time you go through the SQ Process you will keep finding something new.

Please don't put these practices on any 'should-do' list. There is no point in beating yourself up if you let a regular practice slide. The ten steps are not designed to be a chore but to provide you with a sanctuary – one for you to return to when you need some space and stillness from the pace and demands of your everyday life. They will support and hold you when life gets tough and guide you when you are looking for more than the material world can offer.

They are our best teachers; the more we sit with them, the more they reveal to us. Show them some enthusiasm and patience and they will lead you to the same pool of timeless and infinite wisdom that all the greatest spiritual teachers throughout time have tapped into.

This is an ongoing adventure. Exploring and discovering the

wonders of you and the magic of life is best done with a light touch, a childlike curiosity and a sense of fun.

*Life is a song, sing it.*
*Life is a game, play it.*
*Life is a challenge, meet it,*
*Life is a dream, realise it.*
*Life is a sacrifice, offer it.*
*Life is love, enjoy it.*

– Sai Baba

# Further Reading

If you are interested in exploring any of the spiritual traditions further, I highly recommend any books written by the authors below. The books I have listed are simply my personal favourites.

- Adyashanti, *The End of Your World* (Sounds True, 2010)
- Julia Cameron, *The Artist's Way* (TarcherPerigee, 1992)
- Joseph Campbell, *The Hero with a Thousand Faces* (New World Library, 2012) and *The Power of Myth* (Bantam Doubleday Dell, 1989)
- Deepak Chopra, *Ageless Body, Timeless Mind* (Rider, 2008)
- Ram Dass, *Be Here Now* (Crown Publications, 1971)
- Thich Nhat Hanh, *No Mud, No Lotus* (Parallax Press, 2015)
- Michael Harner, *The Way of the Shaman* (HarperSanFrancisco, 1992)
- Hermann Hesse, *Siddhartha* (Penguin Classics, 2008)
- Dzongsar Jamyang Khyentse, *What Makes You Not a Buddhist* (Shambhala Publications, 2008)
- His Holiness the Dalai Lama, *How to See Yourself As You Really Are* (Rider, 2008)

- Marcela Lobos, *Awakening Your Inner Shaman* (Hay House UK, 2021)
- Ramana Maharshi, *Who Am I?* (Sri Ramana Asram, 2008)
- Osho, *Fear* (St Martin's Griffin, 2012)
- Larry Peters, *Tibetan Shamanism* (North Atlantic Books, 2016)
- Matthieu Ricard, *The Art of Mediation* (Atlantic Books, 2011)
- Sogyal Rinpoche, *The Tibetan Book of Living and Dying* (Rider, 2008)
- Rupert Sheldrake, *The Science Delusion* (Coronet, 2020)
- D. T. Suzuki, *Studies in Zen* (Mandala, 1986)
- Lao Tzu, *Tao Te Ching* (Hackett Publishing, 1993)
- Alberto Villoldo, *Dance of the Four Winds* (Destiny Books, 1994) and *The Four Insights* (Hay House, 2007)
- Alan Watts, *You're It* (Sounds True, 2010 [audiobook]) and *Tao: The Watercourse Way* (Random House, 2002)
- Ken Wilber, *A Brief History of Everything* (Shambhala Publications, 2017)

For those who would like to delve deeper, below are details of the studies I refer to in the book:

- Steve Bradt, 'Wandering mind not a happy mind', *The Harvard Gazette*, 11 Nov. 2010
- Carrie D. Clarke, 'How gratitude actually changes your brain and is good for business', Thrive Global, 7 Feb. 2018

- Alyson Gausby, 'Attention spans', *Consumer Insights*, Microsoft Canada, 2015
- Margaret M. Hansen, Reo Jones and Kirsten Tocchini, 'Shinrin-yoku (forest bathing) and nature therapy: A state-of-the-art review', *International Journal of Environmental Research and Public Health* 14.8 (2017): 851
- Ye Wen, et al., 'Medical empirical research on forest bathing (Shinrin-yoku): A systematic review', *Environmental Health and Preventive Medicine* 24.1 (2019): 70

# Acknowledgements

Thank you to Carolyn Thorne for believing in the book, for her gentle wisdom and for her guidance and encouragement throughout. I would also like to thank Holly Whitaker for steering the book through production and all the team at Yellow Kite, including everyone in Sales and Marketing, Design and Production. Thank you to Julia Kellaway for her eagle eye and copy-editing skills, and Euan Thorneycroft at AM Heath and Zoe King, who not only made this book happen, but was an invaluable support from start to finish. I would also like to thank Kate Reardon, Esther Cayzer-Colvin, Fiona Curtis, Tommy Bowlby and D-J Collins.

I am indebted to Alberto Villoldo, PhD, for introducing me to Shamanism and for his continued guidance and friendship. I am also indebted to Geshe Dorji Damdul, who opened the Buddhist way to me and showed great patience and kindness with my endless questions.

Finally I would like to thank Don Martin Piñedo, Don Umberto Soncco Quispe, Don Pascual Apaza Flores, Don Guillermo Soncco Apaza and the late Maestro Edinson Panduro Rumayna for their guidance, support and friendship over the years.

# About the Author

Jo Bowlby is a shaman and spiritual coach to many of those at the top of their game. Over the last thirty years she has trained in various traditions, including: North and South American Shamanism, Tibetan Buddhism, Bön Shamanism, Zen, The Yoga Sutras, Sanskrit, Qigong and holds a black belt in Shotokan Karate.

She studied psychotherapy and counselling at Regent's University in London and is certified in NLP and Hypnotherapy. Jo is a graduate of The Four Winds Society specialising in the traditional teachings and energy work which has been used by Native American and South American shamans for thousands of years.

After graduating, she continued her training in Peru with the Q'ero elders (Inka Shaman) in the Andes and the medicine men in the Amazon rainforest.

Jo has an international client base which means she divides her time between her practice by Battersea Park in London and travelling. She also runs bespoke healing journeys in Peru.

yellow
kite

# books to help you live a good life

Join the conversation and tell
us how you live a #goodlife